The Ghos
t
the Lake District

Tony Walker

Illustrations by Adam Clarke

The White Rabbit Press
1999

The Ghostly Guide to the Lake District
ISBN 0 9534745 0 X
First Published 1999

Published in the UK by The White Rabbit Press
23 Castle Terrace, Penrith, Cumbria, CA11 7DY

Printed by Cerberus Printing
Kirkby Stephen, Cumbria, CA17 4QD

Contents

For Catrin, Imogen and Melanie

The Ghostly Guide to the Lake District

Introduction

This book is a guidebook to the ghosts and haunted places of Cumbria which, if the suggested itineraries are followed, will allow you to visit haunted sites and stay in haunted rooms. It doesn't guarantee that you'll see a ghost; it merely directs you to places that others claim to have seen one.

Each one of the itineraries should take you about a day to complete. Though I give directions in the text, it's a good idea to have a map with you.

Some of the stories told in this book are legends that are centuries old, but many of the accounts of ghostly encounters were only months, or in one case, hours old at the time of writing.

Cumbria is a large, varied and very beautiful English county. Part of it's well known as The Lake District - the region of the Lake Poets, Swallows and Amazons and Beatrix Potter. Millions flock here and the beauty of the Lake District speaks for itself, but there's more to Cumbria than this central area. A secondary purpose of this book is to show you the little visited parts of the County.

To our ancestors the world was mysterious and haunted by spirits of all sorts. On a bright day in a city centre, that might be hard to believe, but when you hear the wind in the trees on a dark night, or see moonlight on a frozen lake, the Otherworld is much closer.

A tour of sites where people swear they have seen or heard supernatural beings seems one way of reconnecting with this fleeting sense of magic. I have not attempted to explain the recorded experiences in any rational way; if people told me they had seen a ghost, and I believed they were sincere, I included their story. This book isn't for the scientific investigator; it's for romantics attracted by gothic ruins and flickering candles.

Something needs to be said about the different kinds of creatures that are in this book. While some seem to be spirits of the dead lingering on, but there are also experiences that seem to be a replay of past events, where the viewer watches but can have no effect.

Another group is the mischievous creatures that prod people in the back and move things around. Traditionally, these creatures are d*obbies*, a kind of Cumbrian leprechaun. They can appear as lights or columns of fire - or even heaps of earth. They don't seem to be spirits of the dead, but rather some kind of non human life form.

The final genus of supernatural beings is the boggle. Boggles are usually animal spirits. They're not very intelligent and can be malevolent. In Cumbria, many appear as black dogs, but they can be pigs or cows and, on occasions, swell to huge size and pursue people across the countryside.

When should you come? Ghosts don't seem to like long summer days, so I would recommend the Autumn, Winter or Spring. Halloween would be a good choice, so would Christmas and New Year. Popular amongst witches might be Beltane (beginning of May). One date you might not have thought of is St Mark's Eve - 24 April. On this night in Cumbria, and in much of the rest of the North of England, the spirits of those due to die in the forthcoming year pass through the porch of the parish church. If you're a visitor to the area, you probably won't see yourself.

You may have heard that Cumbria has a bad climate. Parts of the County do indeed see a little rain. There are also blankets of fog that shroud the moors, blizzards that block mountain roads and sea mists which hang over the coastal marshes. For spotting ghosts, this kind of climate is a distinct advantage.

Before closing, I would like to admit my indebtedness to my sources. Many of the printed ones, be they books, leaflets, or histories compiled by individuals and otherwise unpublished, are listed at the back. They can provide further details on aspects of the things covered in this book. In addition to my gratitude to the authors of the printed material, I would like to thank all of the hoteliers, staff and owners who took the time to talk to me about their ghosts. Last but not least, all of those members of the public who telephoned me, or otherwise sought me out, to tell me of their personal experiences. Very sincere thanks to all of you.

All that remains is to read the book; I hope you enjoy it.

Tony Walker
Penrith
31 October 1998

The Upper Eden Valley

Hotel: The Edenhall Hotel

The Spirit in the Mirror

Tel. 01768 881454

Tariff (1999): B&B from £40

Getting There:

Train: West Coast Main Line to Penrith.
Bus: To Penrith, then check for buses to Langwathby. Cars can be hired at Penrith. Call the Tourist Information Centre (01768 867466) for details. They will also advise you on local buses.

Driving: M6 to Junction 40. Turn onto A66 in direction of Appleby. Come off at first roundabout onto A686 towards Alston. Look out for right turn after 3km signed for Edenhall. Keep on road through village. Edenhall Hotel on your left.

The hotel stands slightly back from the side of the road. If you arrive in daylight, you'll see that it's composed of two distinct sections; the older part's to the left and the modern part, built in the 1960s, is to the right.

Edenhall Hotel was originally an eight bedroomed house called Woodbine Cottage, but it's been a hotel for some years. Once you are inside the hotel you'll notice curious joins; as if the place has been stitched together from various parts. The truth is that it's been much extended over the years. At the very heart of the house is a steep staircase where the low doors and dark wood show that this part's extremely old. In the small lounge by the stairs there's a fireplace with a dark wood surround. The wood

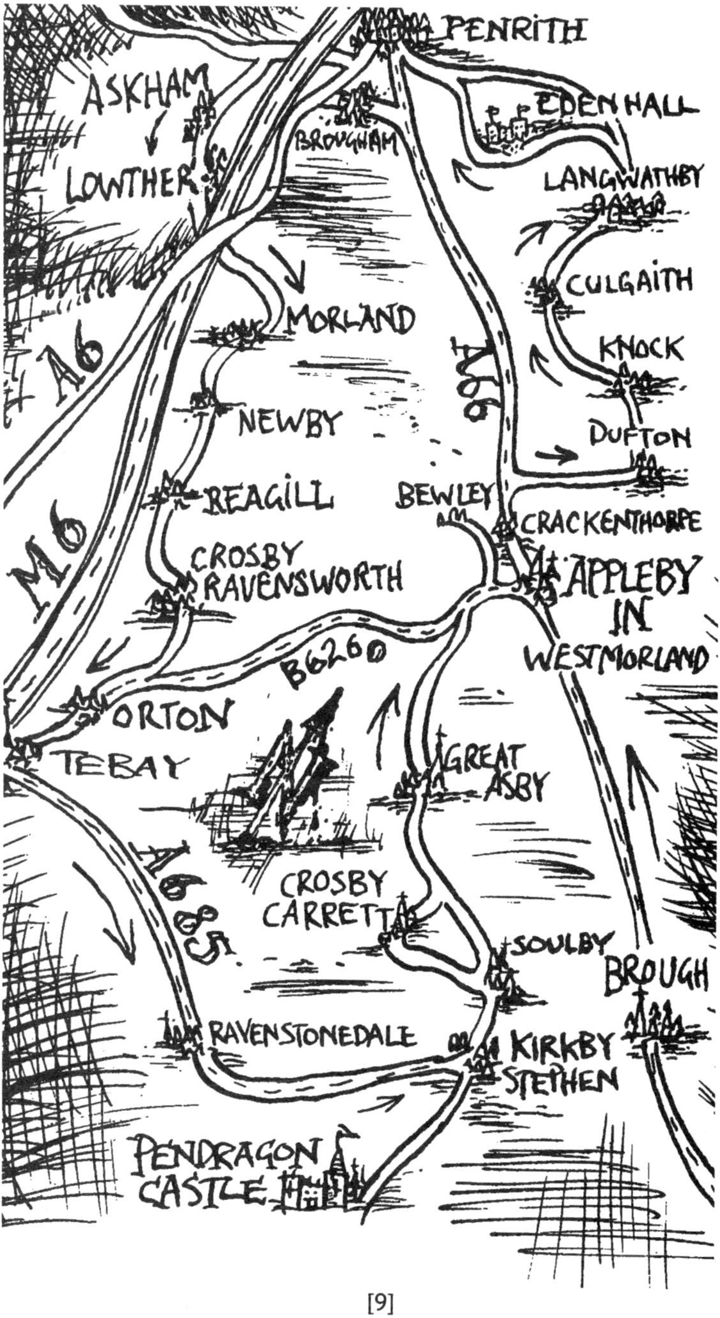
PENRITH
ASKHAM
EDEN HALL
BROUGHAM
LOWTHER
LANGWATHBY
CULGAITH
MORLAND
A66
KNOCK
A6
NEWBY
DUFTON
REAGILL
BEWLEY
CRACKENTHORPE
M6
CROSBY
RAVENSWORTH
APPLEBY
IN
WESTMORLAND
B6260
ORTON
TEBAY
GREAT
ASBY
A685
CROSBY
CARRETT
SOULBY
BROUGH
RAVENSTONEDALE
KIRKBY
STEPHEN
PENDRAGON
CASTLE

is scarred and the decoration Jacobean in style. There are no nails holding it together, only wooden pegs, and this central area of the house may well date from the mid 1600s. Upstairs the floors are slightly uneven and along the ceiling of the corridor there are green glass portholes through which you can dimly see skylights in the roof above.

At first Edenhall only had a club licence for serving alcohol and catered to fishermen using the nearby River Eden, but over the years the fishing rights were sold and this trade lessened. In the 1950s the hotel was owned by two old ladies.

Since then it's been in various hands. The previous owner still lives locally. She told me that some years ago an elderly lady stayed in the hotel. This lady suddenly said that there were three ghosts in the hotel - two women and a man. The owner recalled that one morning shortly after that she and one of the maids went up to Room 38 to make the bed. They thought the room was empty so they went in without knocking, but apologised when they saw a figure standing there. They hastily backed out and they looked at each other. The owner quickly asked the maid if she was sure the previous night's resident had checked out. She was, so they knocked on the door. There was no answer. When they went in again there was no one there.

In November 1997 the Hotel was bought by two business partners. One of them, Richard Burton, set about converting the attics of the original house into bedrooms because he thought they'd provide a good bolt hole - removed from the bustle of the hotel, but still close enough to be on hand if the situation warranted it. When he mentioned this plan to the locals in the bar one night, they gently tried to dissuade him. They said nothing against the attics; just suggested that some other part of the hotel might be a better bedroom for him.

But the work went ahead. The only slight hint that perhaps the attics weren't the best place to relax came from one of the carpenters working on the conversion. All he said was that he always felt uncomfortable when he was alone working up there; as if someone were watching him.

In due course, the job was finished and Richard moved his bed into the left hand attic at the top of the stairs. The room's small and the ceiling slopes down low on either side. There's a skylight and curiously small trapdoors in each of the walls. The trapdoors allow access to the attics and then through to the older parts of the house.

Richard only stayed in that room for five weeks and then had to move out.

Work patterns in the hotel business mean that the best time to snatch some sleep is during the afternoon, between the times for preparing lunch and dinner. Often at this time of day, just when he was about to fall asleep, Richard would have the strong sensation that someone had walked by him in the room; he felt the air move as someone passed and looked up to see the door closing, though he'd not been aware the door had opened. In fact, most times he was pretty certain it had been closed.

He said, 'I never saw anyone but I had the strong visual image of an elderly, but still sprightly, old lady in a long Victorian or Edwardian apron walking past. I felt it was her full dresses moving by that caused the draft of air. It didn't matter whether it was night or afternoon, if I started to fall asleep; she was there.'

It's hard to know who the elderly lady is. She's never been described as being hostile or unkind, merely watchful. It's possible that she was once a housekeeper at the hotel and, even now, likes to keep an eye on what goes on there.

Sally, now in her seventies, worked at the Edenhall Hotel for twenty years. In her day, the attics were used as bedrooms for the bar staff. She remembers that they complained it was very eerie up there. She's in no doubt that the hotel's haunted because she saw the ghost. One day, she was climbing the stairs to the attic, and she saw a woman going up in front of her. She thought it was Irene, one of the maids, but when she got to the attic, there was no one about and certainly no one had passed her coming down.

But it isn't just in the attic bedrooms that a presence is felt. In the bar there used to be a large mirror on the opposite wall from the bar counter. Richard noticed that when he was talking to people standing at the bar, at any time of the day, but particularly in the mornings when the hotel was quiet, just at the edge of his vision he saw a reflection in the mirror as if someone was walking past him. When he turned round, no one was ever there. In the end the mirror was removed.

Richard wasn't the only one who felt or saw something in the bar. Around the same period, one of the waitresses was alone there one morning. She looked up from her tidying and saw an old lady sitting in an armchair in the corner. She was surprised to see a guest at that time, but went about her work. When she looked again, the old woman had vanished.

This ties in with what the previous owner told me; she knew nothing of Richard's experiences, but in the course of conversation she said one day she'd been in the bar when she saw a man in a suit walk across the room carrying a pint. When she turned round he was gone. Who the ghost in the bar is, nobody knows. He seems a respectable enough chap; all he wants is to be left alone to have a quiet drink.

As suggested above, the tales of the haunting of Edenhall Hotel go back further than Richard Burton's time. Room 25 is one of the smallest rooms and isn't normally let to guests unless the hotel is otherwise full. It was previously used as a bedroom for staff and in the early 1990s, there was a waiter living in that room who suddenly left without giving a reason. When the room was cleaned out, it was discovered that he'd put cloves of garlic against the windowpane.

In the course of my research, I contacted a young woman called Teresa who worked at Edenhall in 1990. She told me that there was indeed a room that was known to

be haunted. I wasn't surprised to hear her describe Room 25. She said there was a sunken bath in that room and behind it a mirror. A number of guests had told her that a white apparition of a woman would come out of the mirror when they were in the bath. Sometimes, if guests woke in the middle of the night, they'd find her sitting at the bottom of their bed, just watching them in the dark.

There were certain people who always requested to stay in that room. In the 1980s the local MP, (later Lord) William Whitelaw had aides who came with him to Cumbria from London. One of them always stayed in Room 25. Teresa says he made no secret of the fact that he wanted to see the woman from the mirror again.

The mirror itself and the bath are fairly modern, but the bathroom appears to have been converted from a corridor. The wall behind the mirror is new but it's on the dividing line between the old house and the new. It's well known that ghosts are often seen around boundaries in time or space - walls, doors, anniversaries, midnight or the division between summer and winter that we now call Halloween.

Edenhall

To begin your itinerary after staying at the Edenhall Hotel - perhaps after a disturbed night's sleep - come out of the hotel and turn right. You can walk the first leg to the church, but you'll have to come back for a car if you want to complete the rest of the route by nightfall.

After turning right out of the hotel, stay on the road for a short while. You'll also see a War Memorial in the shape of a Celtic cross to your right as the road bends round. On the left, opposite the Memorial, there's a small road. This leads to St Cuthbert's church, which, though not haunted, is a pleasant and historic place.

The lane to the church passes some lovely cottages and a lodge. You'll see a preaching cross to your left, again of the Celtic wheeled type but actually Tudor in date.

Eventually the road comes to the church and stops. The church is dedicated to St Cuthbert.

In 875 the Danes invaded the kingdom of Northumbria on the east coast. At that time, the bones of Saint Cuthbert were a prized relic of the Northumbrian Christians and they wanted to preserve them from the pagan Vikings. The monks began a hazardous crossing over the Pennines from the east to the west coasts. The fleeing monks eventually came to the Irish Sea at St Bees, from where they planned to set sail and find refuge in Christian Ireland. At every point where they rested on their journey, a church was dedicated to Saint Cuthbert.

No parts of the existing church at Edenhall date from the Ninth Century, but the story might still be true. The church stands alone away from any village and this is often a sign that it was founded on an ancient pagan site. The old pre Christian Celts who lived in Cumbria had various gods and believed in spirits of places - of rocks and rivers and wells. This is why you'll often find churches in the middle of nowhere - they weren't built to serve a local congregation, but originally to honour the god of that place.

Return back down the lane from St Cuthbert's church to the T junction. Turn left and go in the direction of Penrith. Go past the solidly built walls of the home farm. The road bears round left and then you'll see tall gate posts flanking an impressive looking drive. By the side of the gate posts is the South Lodge of what was Musgrave Hall. This building in itself is impressive, so the Hall, which burned down in 1934, must have been grand indeed. The drive is private.

The Musgraves were associated with Edenhall from the late 1400s. Their coat of arms is a ring held by two armoured arms and is carved on the top of the gate posts. Though the Musgraves came to Edenhall in the Fifteenth Century, their most famous possession was quite a bit older. In the estate grounds is St Cuthbert's Well.

Saints of the Celtic church like St Cuthbert have many

holy or magical wells in Cumbria, and indeed all over the west of Britain and Ireland. Back in the Middle Ages, a servant of Edenhall was sent out to fetch water from the Saint's well. As he approached the well he came across a group of the fair folk dancing and making merry. He got closer and he saw that they were in a ring around an enamelled glass vase. He rushed forward and seized it before they could stop him and held it so they couldn't get it back. Finally, giving up in their attempts to retrieve it, they cursed the glass vase, singing;

If that glass should break or fall
Farewell the luck of Edenhall

So all the fortune of Edenhall was placed in that glass object. Because of that, the lords of Edenhall guarded it well.

Today, it looks as if the luck of the Musgraves and Edenhall has long run out. Musgrave Hall was burned down in 1934 and you'll see the monument in the centre of Penrith to the heir of the Musgraves, who died tragically young in 1861. The line died out. Local people used to say that this was because the Luck of Edenhall had fallen and broken into pieces, but that's not true; in fact you can see the Luck on display at the Victoria and Albert Museum in London where it's one of the top one hundred attractions.

Continue on from the lodge until you come to the junction with the A686. Turn left. Go a short way until you see a small road off to your right. The sign says 'Golf Course'. Take this road. This is locally known as Beacon Edge and there are a number of stories attached to it.

Beacon Edge has a bit of a nasty feel to it. Local folklore says that before houses were built here, it was the place where unmarried mothers brought their babies and left them to die. Nearby is a hill known as Gibbet Hill and it was here that executed criminals were left to rot in their chains. You can't get to it by road now, but in 1775 the young William Wordsworth, later poet laureate, rode by on his horse and came across the carcass of a murderer swinging in chains. He fled away in terror and wrote a poem about it.

The murderer had killed a local butcher who'd been drinking just down the road at a pub called the Cross Keys, which is still there. The drunken butcher was making his way home when he was set upon. The murderer was caught and executed in 1767 so he was probably in a fairly decomposed state when Wordsworth came upon him, though it was the practice to coat the corpse in tar so it would be a long lasting reminder of what happened to murderers.

On dark nights, the spectre of a skeleton hanging on a gibbet has been seen at the spot.

Go along Beacon Edge until you see the thirty mile an hour signs that show you are entering Penrith. Park on the right hand side just after the first left turn (Fell Lane). You'll see a wooden finger post that points the way up Beacon Pike.

Thomas Gray, the poet, visited Penrith in 1769 and he climbed Beacon Pike. He gave a wonderful description of the view from the top, through the clouds, into the jaws of Ullswater. The hill has been planted with trees since that time, but the area around the Beacon's still clear and you can see the mountains above the valley that holds Ullswater - the wolf's lake.

There's a much more recent, and perhaps odder story about Beacon Pike. A local girl called Angela Charlton had a strange experience on the path up to the Beacon when she was a teenager. By coincidence, at that time, she lived in the house where I am writing this now.

Angela would often climb the Beacon when she wasn't at school and it's still a popular local walk. One hot day in August in the mid 1970s, she and a friend set out onto the footpath from Beacon Edge. The walk takes about fifteen minutes and the path has many abrupt angles as it zig zags through the trees. The trees crowd thickly round the path as it climbs over craggy sandstone outcrops. Soon you feel quite apart from the everyday world. It's an odd feeling and you have the impression that someone's watching you from the woods on either side. You go up and up, changing direction and losing sight of the path below and behind you.

As Angela and her friend climbed, they chatted away, but the atmosphere grew increasingly heavy; there was thunder in the air. They'd walked up many times and weren't taking much notice of their surroundings, then they turned a corner and stopped. They both saw it. It was an old fashioned cottage, quite roughly made. Angela says that it was like 'a dwelling from the Middle Ages'. The trouble was they'd never seen a cottage there before. Smoke was coming from the chimney, so someone was at home. Angela says that there was a very uncanny feeling about the place. She looked at her friend and then they fled.

When she next worked up the courage to climb the hill some months later, the cottage wasn't there. Though her friend admitted she too had seen the building at the time, as the years have gone by, she refuses to talk about it.

It's difficult to know what happened. Maybe it was the electricity in the air; it was a hot, thundery day. When people report ghostly appearances, they often say that all sorts of electrical devices go haywire. The hill's made of sandstone, which seems to have some association with 'strange' occurrences.

Come down the Pike and take the road called Fell Lane down into Penrith.

Penrith

Penrith's name is Celtic in origin meaning 'red hill' which refers to the sandstone hill called Beacon Pike. You may have just climbed it. On a clear day at least you can see the Beacon from the town - a square tower with a pyramidal roof among the trees on its top. The tower was originally built in 1719.

The centre of Penrith is dominated by a monument to the son of the local landowners, the Musgraves. Around the Monument the streets snake off and disappear into odd yards and passages, most of which are nicely ramshackle.

St Andrew's Church stands in a square of old buildings near the Monument. There has been a church here for a long time, though the current dedication dates from when Penrith was on the southern border of Scotland in the Middle Ages - St Andrew being Scotland's patron saint of course. The churchyard's almost completely enclosed by tall red buildings that have a Dickensian feel to them. They cluster around, leaning over on you as you stand by the church. Local people say that under the flagstones are buried century upon century of the dead. Be careful where you walk.

You'll notice next to the church some old and weathered grave stones. Two crosses with Celtic designs on them stand at either end of carved grave slabs that are called 'hog back' graves. They call this group of monuments The Giant's Grave, and if you measure the distance between the upright crosses at either end, whoever's buried there must have been tall.

Legend says that he was called Sir Ewen or Hugh Cesario and was a giant who lived in caves on the banks of the river Eamont near Edenhall. The caves themselves have a strange name - Isis Parlis, though no one knows what that means. In 1599 locals thought Sir Ewen had been a 'knight errant' who had fought monsters. At that time there was a story that the grave had been opened and huge bones uncovered.

One explanation is that the giant's grave was that of Owen, king of Strathclyde & Cumbria at the end of the Tenth Century. Owen had associations with the Penrith area and his son Dunmail was the last independent king of Cumbria. Folk memory may have confused this King Owen with another Owen whose father Urien ruled from Carlisle much earlier. This Owen was celebrated by the bard Taliesin - himself the subject of mystery and legend. Owain fab Urien appears in tales of King Arthur, and Celtic legends say that Owain had a magical flock of 300 ravens. When he had the ravens with him, he was always victorious in battle. Birds, especially ravens, make frequent appearances in Celtic myth where they are associated with the gods and can travel to the Otherworld.

Whether the Giant's Grave is really that of one of Cumbria's Celtic kings is unknown but the churchyard certainly has an atmosphere; especially if you stand there alone after dark and listen to the wind in the trees and feel eyes watching from the dark windows of the buildings above.

Close to the centre of town, on the other side of the road from the George Hotel, is the Narrowgate Coffee Shop owned by Angela Trowbridge and Louise Hanson. This coffee shop has a ghost called the White Lady.

Back at the turn of the century, the front half of the coffee shop was a laying out parlour; a woman called Mrs White ran it. When the place was being refurbished in 1996, the electricians went down to a cellar which had been sealed off. There they found an original dirt floor which might go back to medieval times. Strangely there was a mound of loose earth in the corner. The electricians didn't like going there; their inspection lamps would keep going out and they had to replace countless bulbs.

In the coffee shop itself the electrics still behave very oddly; lights come on and coffee machines go on when they've definitely been switched off. The situation has got to the stage that at closing time there are always two staff that go around and check after each other. No one's ever left there on their own.

The cellar's entered through a trap door which is weighed down under one of the tables.

Look out for the signs for the M6 Motorway. Don't go onto the Motorway but once you get to the roundabout follow the signs in the direction of Appleby. This will take you to another roundabout which is near Penrith Hospital. Take the A6 road in the direction of Shap. Very soon you'll cross a bridge over the River Eamont.

Go through this collection of houses and continue down the A6. Look out for signs for Brougham Hall on your left. Take the left turn just as you are leaving Eamont Bridge and after a short while you'll find yourself passing a magnificent medieval fortress called Brougham Hall.

Brougham

There's a car park opposite the entrance. Inside the Hall itself is a cafe and interesting shops. Brougham Hall has some stories to tell; the notice board outside explains that this area has been settled from prehistoric times.

Brougham Hall was built about 1480 but reached its zenith in Victorian times when it was known as the 'Windsor of the North' because of frequent visits by Edward VII and George V. It almost became derelict after the 1930s, but has been undergoing a prolonged period of restoration.

Nearby Brougham Castle was the site of the Roman fort and town called Brocavum. A carved stone Celtic head was recovered from the Romano-British cemetery there.

Brougham Hall itself had a guardian skull, similar to others mentioned in this book from Threlkeld and Calgarth. Like these others, it had a niche in the wall and would not tolerate being moved. If it were moved, it would always find its way back to its normal resting place. Furthermore, while it was away various accidents and misfortunes would happen at the Hall. They tried to bury it away from the Hall, but strange noises and groans were heard in its absence. Finally, it was bricked into its niche so that it would remain there in peace.

But that wasn't the end of the skull. In 1989, Mr

Christopher Terry was carrying out extensive restoration work on the Hall and he found the skull in a niche near the bottom of a large wall. He took it to his local dentist who gave the opinion that it was the skull of a man who was aged around 35 when he died. He died from a blow to the head. The skull has never been carbon dated, so we don't know its actual age; it could be medieval, but it could be far older and, if that's the case, then it's possible that he was a sacrificial victim. However, local tradition has it that he was a soldier and there's a poem inscribed at Brougham Hall which reads:

Unknown Soldier from a sunlit shore
Who paid the price in an unknown war
For an unknown god in an unknown time
May peace eternal now be thine
Pray lie within this ancient wall
And guard that it should never fall

Mr Terry is a believer in tradition and he put the skull in a ceramic cooking pot with some other associated bones and some modern coins. He then used a strong adhesive to glue the lid on. After that, the pot with the skull in it was put back in a niche in the wall and sealed in. He refuses to reveal the new resting place of the skull.

Eamont Bridge

When you leave the Hall, return the way you came and, at the road junction, turn right towards Eamont Bridge. Look out for the earthwork in a field to your left. This is called King Arthur's Table, but actually dates from prehistoric times. It's since suffered - the A6 knocked a corner off it when it was built. In the 1500s it was reported to be rather impressive: there were then two entrances to the henge. One was later destroyed by the building of the minor road to the north (not the A6). In Tudor times this entrance had two standing stones flanking it. There used to be a smaller stone circle about 150m to the south of this one, but it's now disappeared under new houses.

One point of interest is that until the 19th Century, communal games were held at King Arthur's Round Table at certain times of the year. Though there's no evidence, it's certainly very possible that these games went back in an unbroken tradition to the rituals of the Stone Age.

Take the left turn by the side of the henge that leads to Yanwath and Pooley Bridge. You can see Mayburgh Henge in the field to your right - it's the large mound with trees growing on it. Look out for the minor road to your right just before the modern bridge. A small sign points down to Mayburgh Henge. Take this road.

The henge is visible as a large mound in a field to your right. If you park here you can go over the broken stile and through a field full of cows to get to the monument. It's quite unusual in that it's still surrounded by banks, and has a standing stone in the middle.

The entrance to the henge is due east of the standing stone. This monolith once belonged to a circle of stones within the henge. In 1725 we have a report of two circles of 'huge' stones within the henge. The centre was once ploughed and this uncovered a number of axes - one bronze and the others stone. It's thought Mayburgh was built about the same time as Long Meg and her Daughters, the major stone circle near Little Salkeld not far away.

Turn round on this dead end road, and when you get to the junction, turn right. This takes you above the Motorway. Go on until you get to Yanwath, then just after the bridge over the railway, take the turn in the direction of Askham.

Askham

Askham is a pretty little village with a pub called the Punchbowl on the way out to Lowther. Though the present owner isn't convinced, a number of her staff report that they have seen a strange shadow man about the pub. He is especially to be found in the bar at the end of the evening, or before the customers arrive on dark winter nights. At certain times he solidifies into a black figure, but there are never any real features to his face or clothes.

From the car park of the Punchbowl, turn right in the direction of Lowther. As you descend to the river, you'll see a church on your right. In the early 1990s, two local girls were doing a spot of amateur ghosthunting. They went to Askham church after dark with the aid of electric torches. They sat in the pews and switched the light off. They swear that there was a sudden gust of air and, in the darkness, someone sat next to them on the pew.

Lowther

Continue on towards Lowther. You cross the wooded river valley and the public road takes you through the Lowther Estate. The Lowthers have been one of the richest families in Cumbria for most of their history. However, there were one or two spendthrifts who threatened the family fortune.

As you climb from the bridge, you'll see another church on your left, soon after Askham church. This was for the use of the Lowther family, and most of them are buried there.

The magnificent ruin of Lowther Castle is to your right. I spoke to someone recently who had a shock when he saw a face at one of the upper windows. It was broad daylight but he knew the figure was a ghost because the upper storeys don't have floors.

On the right hand side of the road as you leave the parkland, you'll see a curiously propped up tree. Legend says that if the branches of this tree touch the ground, great ill luck will befall the Lowthers. I don't know if they're superstitious but they're obviously not taking any chances.

In 1857 Jeremiah Sullivan wrote about the ghost of

James "Jemmy" Lowther - known as the Bad Lord Lonsdale. James Lowther was rich because of the coal under his land near Whitehaven, but he spent more than he earned and ended up owing money to William Wordsworth's father- a debt he never paid. In life Lowther was the coarsest type of feudal baron, but in death he was worse. At his funeral his ghost knocked down the clergyman praying over his bones and then he started creating all sorts of disturbances on the estate. The Hall became almost uninhabitable and his ghost wandered around it. In the end they had to get a Catholic priest who carried out an exorcism in Latin. There was a long struggle. Eventually the priest won and laid him under a rock called Wallow Crag near Haweswater.

There's also the story of the ghostly coach which heads from Lowther on the road to Penrith. It's said to be pulled by four horses and to career madly along the road as if the devil himself was after it. According to the legend it carries the spirit of one of the Lowthers.

The Lyvennet Valley

Go through Lowther and turn right onto the A6, this time going in the direction of Shap. Cross the bridge over the motorway and take the turning left for Great Strickland. Go on through Great Strickland to Morland. Near Morland is supposed to be an earthwork called Skellow Warle or Skelly Warke.

I couldn't find it on the map and the only similar place name recorded in *The Place Names of Westmorland* by A. H. Smith is an earthwork called Skellaw Hill near Shap which isn't so far away to the south west. Whatever the true location of this story, the name seems to be derived from the word 'skeleton'. In 1827, eleven skeletons were found at Skelly Warke. The mound reputedly covered buried treasure. To an extent, the legend proved true, because some of the skeletons had gold ornaments about their wrists and temples. Before the excavation was carried out the mound was haunted by a 'gypsy' looking man with a dark complexion who would glide among the rocks. After the skeletons were dug up, he was never seen again.

We are now in the Lyvennet Valley, which has many, many earthworks and stone circles. It was obviously an important area in prehistoric times and the Dark Age poet Taliesin referred to it as being the bountiful land of Prince Owain fab Urien, whom we spoke about in reference to Penrith.

There are lots of stories of hauntings clustering around this remote and rural area.

From Morland take the minor road to Newby. When you come to the junction, turn right. You pass a hotel on your left called Newby Hall which dates from Jacobean times.

After the hotel, take the even smaller road to your left. This takes you through the hamlet called Sleagill and then on to Reagill.

If you stop your car near the phone box, you can take a walk on a public footpath round by Reagill Grange. If the stories are true, I wouldn't do it after dark.

From the phone box, walk south west along the minor road out of the village. After a short while you have trees on both sides of the road, then only on the right. Walk on until there's a small stand of trees by the road to the left and look out for a footpath just by these. This takes you down a lane towards Reagill Grange.

Gerald Findler in his book, *Ghosts of the Lake Counties*, notes the words of an earlier writer, I S Bland, who wrote about haunting associated with the many earthworks hereabouts. In 1910 a Major White lived at Reagill Grange. Near the Grange there was a gate that opened itself for the traveller late at night and then closed after him. At other places nearby, a figure was supposed to suddenly appear, pass by and vanish. Sometimes it was in the form of a dog, a black calf, a black pig, or even a woman in white. The figure would swell to enormous size and pursue the traveller.

One midnight, Major White was returning to Reagill

Grange on horseback and was near the beck. He saw something white in a nearby tree, and having his gun with him, in the manner of country gentlemen then and now, went to shoot it. As he fired, it began to swell and grew bigger and bigger until it took the form of a woman in white. She jumped onto the horse behind him and terrified the horse so it galloped through fields and hedges at a terrible speed. Suddenly, she disappeared and he got home, his clothes ripped to shreds and his horse flecked with foam.

Go back to your car and leave Reagill by the small road you previously walked down. Take the first left after the lane down to Reagill Grange. You come to a T junction. Turn left here to Crosby Ravensworth. Just after you turn left, you can see the hummocks of a prehistoric settlement in the field on the left hand side of the road. This area really has a very dense collection of stone circles and ancient settlements as the Ordnance Survey map will show you. If you have an interest in these and want to wander the hills to see them, you should consider getting hold of a copy of John Waterhouse's *Stone Circles of Cumbria*, where he discusses each one in detail.

The ghost writer, Elliott O'Donnell wrote about an experience he had in one of these 'druid's circles' round here. While he was in the circle he became aware of an unpleasant smell of death and the feeling that someone was approaching. He slipped out of the circle and hid. From his hiding place he saw a grey figure glide from the nearby wood and go to the largest stone, whereupon it vanished.

Come down to Crosby Ravensworth, with its church and the River Lyvennet flowing through it. To the left as you enter, are the now unremarkable mounds that show that this is an old village; it was once one of the royal lands of Cumbria. Since then history seems to have passed it by. When you come to the T junction, turn left, so that you can see the church and the centre of the village.

There's a story that says that when the Threlkeld family lived at the Hall at Crosby Ravensworth, they kept their valuables in the great pele tower and that the tower was guarded by a huge white bull. It's said the spirit of the bull can still be seen on guard outside the tower on occasions. The Hall has its own 'dobbie' or spirit, which may or may not be the same as the bull. The dobbie revealed to a local farmer the place where he could find buried treasure, but also told him the time and manner of his death. Both of which proved true.

To carry on to Orton, turn round from the church and head south, passing the road you came in on to your right. Continue on until you climb up to the bleak limestone moorland. Carry on up over the moor with limestone pavements on either side until you join the B6260. Turn right to Orton.

Orton has its own boggle which hasn't been seen for some time. In the middle of the last century it was obviously proving rather troublesome because the locals got a Methodist preacher to exorcise it. However, in the middle of his speech, he got a whack on the back of his head from an invisible hand. He gave up the exorcism and left.

Tebay

Continue on through Orton towards Tebay. From the roundabout, go into the village of Old Tebay. There's an inn here called the Cross Keys.

Tebay is famous for its witch, Mary Baynes. Mary had various magical powers. She was reputed to have second sight and had visions of horseless carriages travelling at great speed over the fell. Looking down from Tebay to the M6, it seems that she saw correctly what was going to happen.

Mary was reputedly one of the ugliest women in the country and she fell out with the landlord of the Cross Keys Inn. She had a black cat which wandered onto the land belonging to the Cross Keys and was seized by the landlord's dog and killed. The landlord asked one of his servants to take the cat back to Mary; maybe he was too frightened of her reputation to go himself. The man did as he was told, but when Mary started to read some verses over the dead cat, he obviously thought this was a little over sentimental and exclaimed:

Ashes to ashes
Dust to Dust
Here's the hole
So go you must.

Mary wasn't pleased and she vowed to get her own back on the man. Shortly after he was blinded in an accident.

She died in 1811 at the age of 90, but that wasn't the end of it; in a photograph of the railway taken in 1983 there's a figure of a mysterious cloaked woman who wasn't there when the button was pressed.

Mary's been around the Cross Keys since then and, very recently, there were reports of her getting into bed with sleeping couples and causing mischief.

One other thing about Tebay is that if you look carefully at the houses, you'll see that some of them have rocks with holes in the middle suspended near the doors. This is an ancient Pennine remedy against intrusion by witches and evil spirits. Locally, they are known as dobbie stones.

Leaving Tebay, from the roundabout take the A685 to Kirkby Stephen. This modern road is fast and cuts through some impressive Pennine scenery. It by-passes Ravenstonedale, but this pretty little village has places to eat and is worth a detour.

Kirkby Stephen

Continuing on to Kirkby Stephen, you pass by the station for the famous Settle-Carlisle railway and under the railway itself.

Kirkby Stephen is a town with a very Pennine feel to it. The river that runs through it is the Eden; here close to the start of its journey. In Kirkby Stephen, turn right. There's a small side road, or the larger B6259; both take you towards Mallerstang.

As you continue down this valley which is bleak and little visited, look out for the ruins of Pendragon Castle. The ruined castle stands to the right of the road, just after a turn that would take you back to Ravenstonedale.

This castle is supposed to have been the home of Uther Pendragon, father of King Arthur, who apparently tried, and failed, to divert the River Eden from its course

As well as this, Pendragon is the haunt of mysterious ladies in white, who flit about after dark. It's also the location for fabulous buried treasure, but there's no point going digging for it, because if you do a large black hen will appear, and how ever much earth you dig out in a day, she will have scratched it all back by the next morning.

Turn back on yourself and return to Kirkby Stephen. Just outside the town, you cross a narrow bridge where the Eden foams between rock walls. From here to Kirkby Stephen, the river is haunted by the ghost known as Jingling Annas. Jingling Annas is the ghost of a woman whose manacled hands have been reduced to white bone.

If you listen at the cleft in the rock near the bridge you may also hear the sound of grinding from far below. The story behind this is that in some subterranean lair, the devil is grinding mustard.

You can park in the middle of Kirkby Stephen. Look out for the face of the green man near the tourist information centre in the middle of the town.

The church stands in its own precinct behind rows of stone houses. The green area in front of the church is a nice place to sit down if it's not raining. However, inside the church is the famous Loki Stone.

Like the carvings on the Gosforth Cross over in the west, this stone has a scene from Scandinavian mythology. Here is Loki, bound by the Norse gods as a punishment for his trickery. The stone dates from the 900s. Loki is bearded with horns and is bound by heavy manacles around his wrists and ankles.

The story is that Loki was jealous of Balder the

Beautiful. Because Balder was so precious to the gods, they exacted an oath from all things that grew on the earth - all animals and all stones and metals - that they'd do no harm to him. Loki learned however that the mistletoe, which doesn't grow on the earth, but rather upon other trees, wasn't bound by this oath. Because nothing could hurt Balder, the gods played games of throwing things at him, just to see him remain unharmed.

Loki took a branch of mistletoe and sharpened it. He persuaded the blind god, Hoder, to throw it. The mistletoe dart pierced Balder and he fell dead.

Loki ran away and he changed his shape to avoid detection by the wrathful gods. However, they caught up with him as he swam like a salmon to escape. When they caught him, they bound him beneath the jaws of a venomous snake. As the snake dropped poison on him, he writhed in agony and thus he must remain until Ragnarok - the end of the world and the doom of the gods.

From the car park by the church, turn right onto the A685 in the direction of Brough, but almost immediately take the left turn for Crosby Garrett down a minor road.

Crosby Garrett nestles against the fells behind it, dominated by the viaduct of the Settle-Carlisle railway. It's a village that appears almost untouched by the modern world. As you come in from Kirkby Stephen, you pass by the church to your right. The church was originally supposed to be built at the top of the valley and to this end all the building stone was deposited there. However, one night, the stones were moved by supernatural powers to the top of the hill where it now stands. Taking this as a hint, the villagers built it there.

The modern church building has been added to and remodelled over the centuries, but there's some Anglo-Saxon stonework from the time of Northumbrian rule.

Continue on and turn right after the church. This will take you eventually to a T junction by the railway. Turn right and head towards Soulby. Despite the evocative name, there's nothing mysterious to report here. When you come to the cross roads in the middle of the village, turn left and head along this straight road for quite a while until you come to the junction with the B6260. Turn right towards Appleby.

If you had turned left you would have come to a hamlet called Hoff which is noteworthy because the name marks it as the site of a pagan Norse temple from back in the Viking Age. The farm called Hoff Lunn stands in a wood, which may have been the original sacred grove.

Just as you enter Appleby turn left towards Colby. Once through Colby, continue on for about 2 kilometres and there's a drive which leads to Old Bewley Farm to your left. It's just below the hill where the road climbs to New Bewley Farm.

There's a story about Bewley Castle. There's no public access to the castle itself, but the road there's nice and you are in the real, undiscovered Cumbria here. The original castle was built by Hugh de Beaulieu (hence the name) when he was bishop of Carlisle (1219-1223). There was a chapel inside the castle and church services are still held there on Rogation Sunday.

In the 1500s, Bewley Castle was one of the homes of the Musgrave family. One evening, Sir Richard Musgrave left the castle in the charge of the housekeeper. After he'd gone, and she was about her errands, there came a knock on the door. There was a tall, wild looking woman outside who begged for refreshment. She was given bread and home made beer and fell asleep by the fire.

As the woman slept, the housekeeper had a good look and discovered that it wasn't a woman at all, but a man masquerading as one. The housekeeper could only think that this was some trick that would lead to robbery or murder, so she poured boiling tallow from the candles into the open mouth of the stranger. As the man writhed in pain, the housekeeper rang the alarm bell in the tower.

Sir Richard came rushing home to find the man's robber band fleeing from their hiding places around the castle. The robber was Belted Will Scott, a well known rogue. In fact there's a pub named after him in Hallbankgate, near Carlisle which is haunted.

Appleby

Once the county town of Westmorland, Appleby is well worth a visit. The castle dates from Norman times - once home to Richard III, the infamous child murderer. The ghost of Lady Anne Clifford is supposed to haunt the castle, though none of the current staff have seen her.

Go down the main street of Appleby with its green. There's a cafe and gallery and other places to eat here. There are also nice walks beside the Eden.

There's a story from Appleby about the Old Shepherd. This ghost haunted one of the houses in the town from the late 1600s onwards. He was exorcised by a Catholic priest and expelled from the house and laid under a large stone not far away.

Many years later a group of people were celebrating an election victory and they set a large bonfire close to the stone. Whether the heat did something is difficult to say, but the ghost of the Old Shepherd emerged as a large white shape. He floated around the crowd and then away down to the river. He was so slow that the young people were able to follow him. He disappeared near the water with a splashing sound such as an animal would make. They lit another fire to summon him back and he reappeared, only to disappear again when chased by boys.

Crackenthorpe

Bear right and cross the bridge over the Eden. Turn left and head onto the main A66 dual carriageway in the direction of Penrith. Prepare to turn off right very soon for Crackenthorpe.

There's a story connected with Crackenthorpe Hall. The Hall lies on the left hand side of the A66 by the Eden.

There was a lady called Elizabeth Sleddall or Peg Sneddle (authorities agree that the two are the same woman) who in the time of Oliver Cromwell (1653-1658) married the squire of Crackenthorpe Hall.

Local stories say that Peg was rather unladylike when alive and when dead she was worse. Whenever a head of the family was about to die, she would appear near a local tree called Sleddall's Oak and howl like a banshee. She caused so much trouble with her haunting the hall, that they took her from her grave in the village churchyard and buried her under a boulder of Shap granite in the middle of the Eden. This presumably has something to do with the spirit world's dislike of running water. A Catholic priest was called to perform an exorcism and he commanded her to remain buried under the river for nine hundred and ninety nine years. However, every September she rises up from her watery grave and enters the Hall through a blocked up window.

I was telephoned by a young girl who claimed to have seen her by the side of the River in the mid 1990s near the spot where the stone is.

The Helm Wind, that wind peculiar to the Eastern Fellside, rises from Fiend's Fell when everywhere else in Cumbria's still. When this wind blows Elizabeth Sleddal can be seen driving in a carriage drawn by six coal black horses. The horses have flaming eyes and nostrils and the coachmen wear tricorn hats and black boots.

Turn back onto the A66 in the direction of Penrith, but turn right for Long Marton. From the centre of Long Marton, go under the railway, then turn back on a small road to your right. This will take you to Dufton.

Dufton stands in the shadow of the Pennines and is a long village with a sandstone fountain with a Latin inscription on it. It's a very pretty village and there are one or two places you can stay there. One of these is Dufton Hall. It's actually a working farmhouse, but very historic. The Hall was owned at various times by the Dacres and Howards, then the Earls of Thanet. For a long time it was owned by the Tufton family, who have a pub named after them in Appleby.

When I asked if the hall was haunted, Mrs Howe, the landlady, firmly assured me that it wasn't. I asked her how she could be so definite and she told me that previous owners had taken precautions - they had buried horses skulls underneath the hearths to keep the spirits away. These had been found when new fireplaces were being put in, and had been left in place.

Go on through the village in the direction of Knock. About halfway between Dufton and Knock is an old church dedicated to St Cuthbert that stands alone on the right hand side of the road. Continue on the winding road until you come to the T-junction. Turn left in the direction of Milburn and Blencarn. Continue on through Skirwith and then you'll come into the village of Langwathby. If you turn left here, go over the metal bridge and look out for the cricket field and hut to your left. By this field is a left turn and a sign shows you that the Edenhall Hotel is a short way along this road.

The Lower Eden Valley & The North Pennines

Inn: The Fox & Pheasant

The Woman in Brown

Tel. 01697 472400

Tariff (1999): From £25

Getting There:

Driving: Come off the M6 at Junction 41 (Catterlen). Take the second exit towards Penrith. At the next roundabout turn left onto the A6 towards Carlisle. Keep on to High Hesket and turn right for Armathwaite. In the centre of the village turn right over the River Eden. The Fox and Pheasant is to your right.

Train: Armathwaite is on the Settle - Carlisle line. Trains from Carlisle or Leeds will take you there. The pub's a short walk through the village, over the bridge.
Bus: Check buses from Carlisle on 01228 606000

The Fox & Pheasant is really two buildings: one old and the other very old. It stands on the east side of the broad River Eden, over the bridge from the main village below a thickly wooded slope. It has a square and formal looking red sandstone wing which faces onto the road that was built to try and attract the gentry. Behind it, tucked away, and actually much more charming, is the low whitewashed building which is the traditional Cumbrian inn.

The bar's dark and warm; it has a stone floor, low ceilings, and a blazing log fire. The staff are friendly, the beer's good. It's used by the local farmers and when they're not working out in the cold they must like their

BRAMPTON
HALTWHISTLE
A69
HALLBANKGATE
CASTLE CARROCK
HALTON LEA GATE
LAMBLEY
KNARSDALE
CUMREW
A689
AINSTABLE
GROGLIN
LOW HALL
ALSTON
RENWICK
GLASSONBY
LEADGATE
GARRIGILL
LONG MEG
MELMERBY
HUNSONBY
LANGWATHBY
TO PENRITH

comfort because the seats are luxurious deep leather ones. There's no background music. In fact it's all you could want from a country pub. The current owners are the Starkeys and they have never seen the ghost, but the previous owner, a Mrs Rosser did. On one occasion she and a friend were in the bar when they were astounded to see a woman in brown old fashioned clothes come through the bar door from the other room, ignore them completely, and walk out through the front door. She appeared as solid as anyone else, but when she walked through the front door, she didn't open it.

Other people have seen her in the bar, or at least felt her presence. In 1994 a Welsh lady came to stay at the hotel and she told them that they had a ghost there. Local history has it that the spirit's a lady whose two children were knocked down by the stage coach in the days when the Fox & Pheasant was a coaching inn.

Local lads playing pool have also had visitations from the lady in brown that reportedly made the hair stand up on their necks.

The other ghost at the Fox & Pheasant is seen and felt around Room 3. Many guests have reported strange goings on and electrical devices playing funny tricks in the room. One of the staff, a young girl called Oriol, wouldn't go in there to make the bed without her dog.

It was from the window of Room 3 that a notorious local highwayman was hung after being caught and given a summary trial. Who he was, or when that happened, I haven't been able to find out.

Armathwaite is the site of one the few bridges over the River Eden. The Eden features quite a lot in local history and was mentioned by Roman geographers. There's a line in Old Cumbrian poetry dating from the Sixth Century where it's described as running "too wine coloured" with the blood of the Cumbrians and their enemies who died at a battle at a ford.

The name Armathwaite itself is Norse and shows that once upon a time a hermit came to find solitude there.

The banks of the Eden both up and down river from Armathwaite were good for hermits because the soft sandstone cliffs have natural caves that were easily extended to form rough sorts of dwellings.

In the 14th Century, north Cumbria became the fashionable setting for tales of King Arthur, who, according to these stories, had his court at Carlisle. In one of the stories - *The Adventures of Arthur at Tarn Watheling* - Sir Gawain jousts with a Scottish Knight who later joins the Round Table. Tarn Watheling, a small lake now drained, was near Armathwaite. It's now a wood.

The area around here was for centuries a thick forest known as Inglewood. There was a mighty tree in this forest called the Court Thorn near High Hesket that existed as late as 1773. On St Barnabas' Day, The Court of the Forest was held around the tree. St Barnabas' Day is 11 June, and before the calendar was changed, this was the longest day. We see here the survival of very old customs, perhaps as old as the remains of the stone circles that dot this area. The association we find with Sir Gawain who fought the Green Knight, The Court of the Forest and the ancient and once almost impenetrable Inglewood, makes one start thinking of Green Men - the living spirit of the plant kingdom.

Cumrew

From the Fox & Pheasant, turn right. Take the left road at the junction which takes you along by the River Eden. Go through Holmwrangle and turn left at the junction. Keep on until you get to Carlatton Mill. Ignore the left turn for Carlisle and take the right past the farmhouse along the straight, tree lined road. This takes you to Cumrew.

You'll see the steep Pennine fellside that begins to tower above you. Cumrew itself is bypassed by the main road and you have to take a detour off it to get into the village proper.

This place hasn't changed much with the passage of

time; a few of the houses have been prettied up, but the rest have the charm of the real countryside. Some of them are very attractive indeed, especially at the south end of the village where farm buildings with toadflax and ivy on their walls lead up to the Victorian church. Sadly, the church is left locked, but the site's very pleasant with trees that sway in the wind blowing from Fiend's Fell.

Behind this hill the land starts to climb. This is the site of the ancient fort known as Dunwalloght which probably dates from the Iron Age, just before the birth of Christ.

Above the fort, there's a large cairn of rocks on the summit of the fell. This is supposed to be the burial mound of an old Celtic chieftain, but could well be much older because when it was excavated it was found to contain cremation burials from the Bronze Age.

Local legend makes this cairn the haunt of ghosts and witches, and for all sorts of reasons - weather included - not the place to venture up to on a dark winter's night.

From Cumrew, get back onto the B6413 and head north (with the fells on your right) through the village of Castle Carrock until you see the signs for Talkin pointing along a lane to the right.

Talkin

Talkin is locally famous for its tarn - a small glacial lake - popular for Sunday walks, but in *The Haunted Pub Guide*, Guy Lyon Playfair mentions the Blacksmith's arms at Talkin. Apparently the doors open and close on their own, pictures fall off the walls and glasses fly across the room in the bar. The story is that the ghost is a previous landlady called Maggie Stobart. You can get food at the Blacksmith's Arms or one of the other pubs in the village.

if you turn right out of the door of the Blacksmith's Arms you'll see a minor road leading off to your right. If you take this fairly straight little road you'll come to the hamlet of Hallbankgate. Turn right onto the A689 in the direction of Alston, but as you do so, you'll see on the corner a pub called the Belted Will.

Hallbankgate

The Belted Will is named after Belted Will Scot, a famous robber in these parts in the 1500s. As you'll remember, Belted Will met a grisly end when he tried to rob Bewley Castle near Appleby. This pub in Hallbankgate has been troubled by a ghost in the past and the previous owners, who were called Mordue, would often talk about it to the villagers. Since they left, the pub has been run by a local family who profess never to have had any odd experiences and say the whole thing's a load of rubbish.

Continue down the A689 in the direction of Alston. You'll soon begin to get an idea of the bleak grandeur of the North Pennines. Pass the off-puttingly named hamlet of Midgeholme and, as you leave the hamlet, you'll see that you are leaving Cumbria and entering Northumberland.

Go on the A689 through Halton lea gate and then look out for a sharp left turn for Lambley. Turn left here and head down until you go over the bridge over the River South Tyne. Follow the road as it bends right and go up the hill through Coanwood until you come to some more houses, the road goes sharply left towards Haltwhistle, but turn onto the minor road between the houses to your right. Follow this road across the fell until it descends towards the river again. You may feel you're going in circles but the views are worth it. At the bottom of the hill turn left and go along until you cross another bridge over the South Tyne. Once over that there's a bridge over a small burn and you'll shortly see the ancient house called Knarsdale Hall on your right.

Knarsdale

The Makepieces, who have renovated the Hall in recent years, tell me that they have had no ghostly experiences since they moved there, but it wasn't always so.

At an indeterminate date in the past, the Laird of Knarsdale was a selfish and irritable man who waited until middle age before marrying. The girl in question was young and pretty and didn't want to marry the Laird, but he was rich and her parents forced her.

Though she married him, the girl didn't submit to his will in everyday matters and things weren't happy. After a while, the Laird became the guardian of a niece and nephew who had been orphaned and he took them into his house. Soon the boy and the Laird's young wife started an affair. They kept this secret, but one night the boy's sister saw them together. Fearful that she might tell the old man, the adulterous couple plotted to murder her.

One dark night the wife woke the Laird and told him the sound of a door banging from one of the outbuildings was keeping her awake. It was a foul night and he was reluctant to go outside. Eventually his wife said that if he wouldn't go, then he should ask his niece to go and shut it. Being the sort of man that he was, this seemed a good option and he called for the young girl to go outside in the storm and shut the door.

When the girl got outside she was grabbed by her brother who was waiting for her in the dark and, after a brief struggle, he overpowered her and drowned her in the nearby river.

After a long while, even the Laird began to feel the pangs of conscience and he asked his wife to get up and see whether the girl had come back. The woman got up and waited in the corridor a while. Then she returned to the marriage bed, and told him his niece was safely back. Convinced that all was well, he fell back asleep. After a very short time, he was wakened by the most horrendous howl and, sitting bolt upright, he saw the ghost of the young girl at the bottom of his bed.

The next day they found that the boy had gone. Not willing to reveal the terrible crime, the wife kept the story to herself but went slowly mad because of her guilt.

Eventually, in her ravings, she gradually revealed what had happened and when the river was searched the body of the girl was found. Despite the Laird's best efforts, the boy escaped the reach of the law.

To this day, on the anniversary of the murder, the wind's supposed to get up and the doors bang and once again the ghost of a soaking wet, howling girl wanders the corridors of Knarsdale Hall.

Continue on past Knarsdale Hall until you rejoin the main road. Turn left for Alston. Alston is the highest market town in England and the road you are now on is the best of the five lonely routes that lead to it over the moors.

Alston

Alston's a small place of about fourteen hundred people with twenty miles of empty moorland on all sides. It stands on a hill and there's an attractive cobbled high street leading up to the main square. It's only here at all because a century or so ago there was lead to be mined in the hills. The lead's gone, but the town remains. The houses are built of a dark limestone. The buildings are old and you can see inscriptions of the dates they were built - 1670, 1659 - on them as you climb the cobbled streets.

There are various pubs. The Angel, the Turks Head and the Bluebell are three of the many pubs and all have warming log fires. There's also a good tea shop and two butchers who vie for the title of best sausage maker in Cumbria. You can also get good locally made honey mustard.

In the winter, Alston can feel like a community under siege from the weather but even then it has its beauty.

The only ghost in Alston is in the town's Cooperative Supermarket, though the staff there are reluctant to talk about it. If you want to hear about spirits then, you must go on to Garrigill.

Garrigill

Continue on through Alston in the direction of Middleton in Teesdale. This road leads over the desolate moors to County Durham - a glorious wilderness of bog and heather,. In Spring, the silence is broken by the plaintive cry of the curlew and in Winter by nothing at all. Turn right down the steep hill into Garrigill.

Garrigill is surprisingly pretty and gentle in the middle of all this emptiness and is said to have the freshest air in England. If you continue left past the George & Dragon you are on road that shortly becomes fit only for feet and horses. Go about fifty yards and look out on your right for Ivy House.

Ivy House

Someone at the Top of the Stairs

Tel. 01434 382501

Tariff (1999): from £16

Ivy House was built in 1609. In the 1850s the famous geologist Westgarth Forster lived there. If you stay here overnight you can almost feel the emptiness of the fells for miles around and imagine the lost spirits that wander in the dark outside. There are stories of witchery around the village, though it's of a nice not nasty kind. There's also someone who walks around the top of the house at the top of the stairs. He's never been seen by the current proprietors, but they hear and feel that he's around. At the top of the stairs there's a door which leads to nowhere. It used to lead to a series of outbuildings, but these have been knocked down and the door now serves no purpose, except perhaps to let the spirit in. Electrical equipment behaves oddly, but otherwise the ghost leaves everyone alone.

Instead of going back to Alston, take the minor road through Garrigill in the direction of the hamlet of

Leadgate. Before you get to Leadgate you pass through an area with a few farms that all called something Dryburn. On this road a man called J W Roddam saw a ghostly horseman in 1918. Apparently the rider was galloping along at full pelt, but the horse went out of control and threw him against the wall. Mr Roddam went over to the rider, but when he got there, both the man and the horse had vanished into thin air. Mr Roddam wrote a poem about this which he published in his book *Memories of the Cumbrian Fells*

You can then continue on from Dryburn to the hamlet of Leadgate. Turn left here and continue until you come to the junction with the A689. Turn left in the direction of Penrith.

This road leads down into the Eden Valley over Hartside Pass and is the 'A' road most frequently closed by snow in England. You'll soon notice the lack of houses. If the snow's falling as you are making your way along this road, be warned that it drifts badly on Hartside and you might be better returning to Alston to wait it out.

You may see grouse here - both red and black, famous or otherwise. Grouse sit through the snow and ice, shivering under the blizzards all winter long. You may also see short eared owls quartering the ground in low swoops looking for prey during the brief winter days.

As you drive, watch out for walls of fog - they're actually low cloud hanging on the face of the hills, but if there's no fog, and it's light, you'll see the stepped profile of Cross Fell to your left. Cross Fell was historically called Fiends Fell until a cross was set up there to drive the demon away.

The lonely building on the bend to your right isn't lived in. It was built as a gaol for prisoners making their way from Durham into Cumbria, much the same route, but much less holy than that taken by the relics of St Cuthbert centuries previously.

After five kilometres or so from the turn from

Leadgate, you'll come to the summit of Hartside Pass. In good weather the view back down over the Eden Valley, the Solway Plain and across the sea to the Scottish mountains is one of the best in Britain. There's also a cafe at Hartside Top, but if you're here in winter it will be closed and empty. You're now going to descend into the Eden Valley on a road of many twists and turns. At Hartside Top you are 1900 feet above sea level but the gradient of the drop is very gentle, a testament to Thomas Telford, the famous engineer who built it.

A particular wind blows along the face of the Pennines. This wind, known as the Helm Wind, mysteriously blows through the villages on what is called the Eastern Fellside of Cumbria. When places like Penrith are dead calm the Helm Wind can blow quite fiercely along the Fellside. Because of this, any snow comes in blizzards and drifts many feet high across the bends in the road. If you get caught in snow, be aware that you are some miles from any inhabited house. You're probably best off waiting to be rescued rather than attempting to walk.

Eventually you arrive at the pretty red sandstone village of Melmerby. The Eden Valley feels like a different world from that of the high Pennines. Melmerby has a relatively famous bakery, a nice post office and a good pub - The Shepherds Arms. It also has a gallery called after the Egyptian goddess Isis. Or maybe it's called after the giant's caves of Isis Parlis, on the banks of the River Eden not too far away.

Keep on the road in the direction of Penrith and after a few kilometres you'll see signs on your right for the interestingly named Robberby. Look for the next right turn after this one.

Take this right turn which is signposted for Hunsonby. Go through Hunsonby, take the left at the fork just after Hunsonby and then on over the cross roads. Turn right at the T-junction and you'll come into the clearing and see the large stone circle known as Long Meg and Her

Daughters.

Long Meg

The nickname Long Meg could well date from the reign of Henry VIII, when the original Long Meg was 'a virago of Westminster'. Afterwards, anything tall and thin, like this standing stone, got the name. But our Long Meg is much older than Henry VIII. She and her Daughters belong to the late Stone Age or early Bronze Age.

You'll notice that the road to the farm cuts through the circle of stones. The stones themselves are impressively large and roughly formed. One tall stone stands to the North West - Long Meg herself. Apparently you aren't able to count the same number of stones twice and if you do, then something ill will befall you. Long Meg has some cup and ring marks carved into her - almost obliterated by time. Cup and Ring marks are found on these kind of monuments in Britain and Ireland. One theory is that they are shamanic in origin. The shamans of many cultures journey to the otherworld in an ecstatic state and in this state of altered consciousness, they reportedly see vortices like these cup and ring carvings.

It's difficult to say why Long Meg was erected, but there are lots of stone age monuments in the Eden Valley. It may have been a cult centre of some kind; human societies only expend such effort in building memorials to gods or rulers, and the longest lasting ones seem to belong to the gods.

Though Long Meg is impressive today, there was more to her and her family in earlier years. In 1599, the historian Camden describes over two hundred stones with two tumuli in the centre. Local tales say that Long Meg and her Daughters were turned to stone for dancing on a Sunday, or that the outer stones were men trying to seduce Meg so that she would give herself to them. As a punishment, everyone, including poor Meg, was turned to stone.

There's also a story that a Colonel Lacy, who excavated

the nearby Lacy's Caves on the banks of the Eden, tried to demolish the circle by blasting. As his men set the charges a strange storm arose and rain fell and thunder rumbled. Lightning snaked across the sky and the workmen, soaked to the skin, looked up in awe. They believed that some force was trying to stop them interfering with Long Meg. They fled and refused to bother her again. So Long Meg and Her Daughters still stand.

And it's still a strange place. In the early 1990s, a local girl called Paula Thompson and her friends decided to do a bit of ghost hunting at Long Meg. Friends had gone there in their cars late at night to sit and talk and do what teenagers do. They reported seeing flashes of light outside the car, coming from the stones. They told Paula and they all decided to go back another night as a group.

It was after midnight and at first Paula wouldn't get out of her car. Her friends teased her and so, reluctantly she opened the door. By that time the others had spread out round the circle. There was some light from the moon, and she walked over to Long Meg, the tallest stone. She saw a dark shape in front of her. As she got closer, it started to move towards her very quickly. She thought it was a male friend having a laugh and called out for him to stop. He didn't stop and she saw that he was going to run into her. As it got closer she saw the shape wasn't her friend. To her horror it ran right through her. She says she felt cold and frightened and rushed back to the car.

Another time a group of people went there late, they met a coven of witches. When you visit Long Meg, you'll more often than not see offerings of flowers or suchlike around Long Meg herself, or hanging in the tree nearby. My advice would be to stay away from Long Meg after dark. These people probably mean no harm, but they don't like to be disturbed.

Continue on to Glassonby and then take the road to Kirkoswald. Kirkoswald is a very pretty village. There's a post office here and several pubs. But after you've refreshed yourself, pass on through the village, bearing right and heading for Renwick.

Renwick lies at the bottom of the Pennine Fellside. It's a small place, and like all the Fellside villages, has the impression of being on the edge of the known world. In 1799 strangers must have been few and far between. In that year it was decided to renovate All Saints Church which had become dilapidated. As workmen pulled down the church prior to rebuilding, they disturbed a monstrous creature; it had the tail of a dragon and the body of a cockerel - a description of the classical Cockatrice that turned men to stone with its glance. The workmen fled and the beast flew over the village, terrifying everyone except one local stalwart called John Tallentyre. Tallentyre cut a bough of a nearby Rowan tree, aware of the Rowan's effectiveness against witches, warlocks and unclean spirits. As he came into the open, the Cockatrice attacked him. He struck it with the magical wood and through the branch's power, he killed it. For his courage he was awarded the ownership of the estate where he'd previously been only a tenant.

That should have been the end of the cockatrice, but even in 1959, it was reported to be seen flying around the village at dusk.

There's a road that runs to the north from Renwick along the bottom of the Fellside. It's a bleak and unwelcoming landscape, especially in winter when the snow piles deep and blocks the small road. There are all sorts of supernatural stories from this edge of civilisation. One of them is perhaps the most compelling of all stories that purport to document the existence of vampires.

Croglin

A few miles along the road you come to Croglin. Near this village is the site of the best 'true' vampire story in British history. In fact the vampire didn't come from the village but rather haunted the nearby Croglin Low Hall and its neighbourhood.

To find Croglin Low Hall, go through Croglin and take the first left. When you come to the cross roads turn left again. You'll pass by the farmhouse known as Croglin High Hall to your left. Croglin Low Hall lies a little further on, to the right. There's no public right of access to Croglin Low Hall and it's still a working farm, so tourists aren't normally able to visit. However, you can stop on the narrow road and look at the Hall from afar as you think about the vampire. It's a lonely place. Not much traffic goes by and I guarantee you'll begin to feel uneasy if you find yourself sitting in your car after dark here.

The vampire story dates from just after the English Civil War. The owners of Croglin Low Hall were a family called Fisher and the story was told to one Augustus Hare by a descendent of the family in 1896. For some strange reason of their own, the Fishers decided to go and live in the south of England and rent out the farm. The tenants they found were two brothers and a sister called Cranswell. The new family stayed in their remote farmhouse through the first winter without event. The summer came and, that year, it was stiflingly hot so they slept with the windows open. At that time the Hall was only one storey high - the upstairs has been built subsequently. Near the Hall was a chapel and a small graveyard which once belonged to the Howard family - great landowners in these parts.

One particular airless summer night the men sat with their sister watching the moon rise. After a time they decided to go to bed.

The sister lay in her bed, the bedclothes cast off because of the heat. She'd closed her window, but not fastened the shutters. She gazed out of her window, propped up on her pillows as the long summer day faded out and night took its place. In Cumbria at midsummer, because it's quite far north, it doesn't get very dark at all between sunset and sunrise

Miss Cranswell soon became aware of two lights some distance from the house in the belt of trees that separated the lawn from the graveyard. She watched and, after a while, could make out a dark shape moving towards the house - towards her window. A terrible horror seized her. She wanted to get up and leave the room, but to go to the door would have meant she had to go closer to the window. Besides she'd locked the door from the inside and so would have to stand there and unlock it - all the while clearly visible to whatever was out there.

Frozen to the spot, she stared at the shape but then it turned and, instead of moving closer to her window, it started to move around the house. She jumped up and ran to the door. Her hands were shaking so much that she found it hard to turn the key. And then her heart nearly stopped. Behind her - close to her though she didn't dare look - she heard a scratching at the window. It was outside. Just feet away. She stood there petrified; still not turning her head. Then she heard the sound of it unpicking the lead that held the glass in place. She forced herself to look and saw one pane of the mullioned glass come away and a long bony hand stretch in and turn the window catch.

Whatever it was, it came in through the window with a rush and grabbed her - its fingers in her hair, its mouth at her throat. It bit her neck and forced her onto the ground. As it bit her she screamed.

Her brothers heard the noise and came and battered at the locked door. The creature looked up and as the door was broken open, then it turned and fled out of the window, leaving her lying on the floor, bleeding profusely from a wound at her neck.

One brother clambered out of the window and went

after it. But it was fast and before he could catch it - perhaps it was lucky for him that he didn't - it disappeared into the blackness around the graveyard.

Trying to explain it afterwards, the girl rationalised that the creature must have been a dangerous lunatic. But she was still horribly shocked and her brothers took her away from Croglin to recover.

They stayed away for a while, but then, as autumn came, it was she who urged them to return to Croglin. They'd paid for the tenancy, and besides, she joked, it would be very bad luck to come across two escaped lunatics in one place.

They returned to Croglin and spent the winter there. She had the same room, but always closed the wooden shutters. The brothers took to carrying loaded pistols with them around the house. Nothing happened until one night in March.

The sister was lying in bed when she heard a terribly familiar scratching at the window. She struggled to get fully awake and scrabbled for a candle and something to light it with. When she got a flame she saw that the shutters were opened. Staring in at her was a brown shrivelled face and she saw its long bony hands picking at the lead of the windows.

She screamed. In an instant, her brothers rushed in with their pistols. She pointed to the window, but the creature had gone. The brothers ran out of the front door and saw it moving across the lawn towards the graveyard. They fired and one of them hit it in the leg. It scrambled away into the darkness and they lost it.

The next day the brothers summoned their neighbours, and with their help they went into the graveyard. The tenants of nearby Croglin High Hall had also been suffering visits from it and their young daughter had bite wounds at the throat. The father had thought she'd been bitten by a rat, but when the Cranswells said what had happened to their sister, they feared the worst and the father joined

the party as it made its way to the graveyard.

One of the locals had heard rumours of a particular vault being home to some monster so they opened it up. They stood around, pistols and other weapons at the ready. The vault was full of coffins but most were smashed and the remains mangled and strewn across the floor. Only one coffin was undisturbed. They lifted the lid and there they saw the mummified and shrivelled figure that had moved as if alive the night before. To confirm what they feared they looked at the leg and found a recent wound from a pistol ball. There and then they set fire to the dry coffin and burnt the vampire in it. In his book *Legends of the Lake District* J. A. Brooks tells that in the early years of this century the tenants of Croglin Low Hall had to deal with a fire in the dining room chimney. When the fire died down and they were rebuilding the chimney, they found an ancient burnt corpse in there. Though the tenant wanted to rebury the corpse in a churchyard with proper Christian rites, he died before he was able to do this. It's possible that the corpse is still there in the chimney.

Back to Armathwaite

To return to the Fox & Pheasant at Armathwaite, go left from Croglin Low Hall drive. Continue on this road, past the farm called Hazelgill to your left and take the next left just before the farm called Cairnhead. Keep on this road until you come to a T-junction. Turn right for Ainstable and go through Ainstable until you get to Armathwaite. The Fox & Pheasant is on your right.

Hotel: Dalston Hall

The Whispering Room

Tel. 01228 710271

Tariff (1999): B&B £175 for double room

Getting There:

Driving: Go to junction 42 of the M6 - just south of Carlisle. The first exit from this roundabout it you were going north and the third if you've been coming south is signposted for Dalston. Take this country road until you come to a junction. Take a right turn for Dalston. Go through the village in the direction of Carlisle and you'll pass the Nestle factory on your right. Shortly after this there's a wood. You'll see a sign for Dalston Hall Hotel pointing right down a lane into the wood.

Train: Catch the train to Carlisle. You can either change there onto the Cumbrian Coast Line and get off at the first stop: Dalston, or get a taxi from outside Carlisle Station. Dalston Hall hotel's about ten kilometres south of the City For buses ring 01228 606000

Dalston Hall dates back to Norman times. At night the towers are floodlit which brings out the orange in the sandstone walls. The hotel's approached up a drive through the trees. Look out for the ghost of the Victorian handyman as you drive up at night; he's often been seen in the grounds.

The current facade of Dalston Hall is actually the most modern part of the building - dating from 1899 - and it hides a more ancient heart. The difference between the daylight outside and the subdued dimness inside is

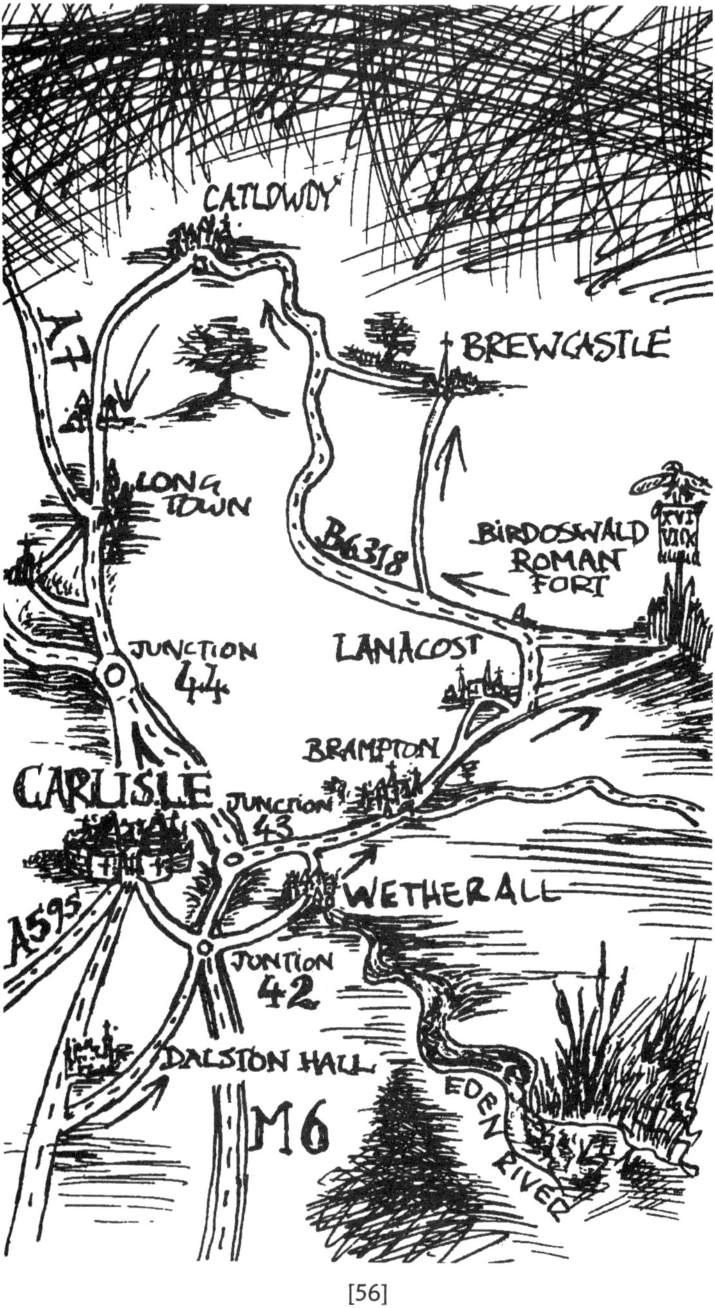

CATLOWDY
BREWCASTLE
A7
LONG TOWN
B6318
BIRDOSWALD ROMAN FORT
JUNCTION 44
LANACOST
BRAMPTON
CARLISLE
JUNCTION 43
WETHERALL
A595
JUNTION 42
DALSTON HALL
M6
EDEN RIVER

notable; all around dark wood panelling makes the place intimate and yet strange. Passing into the hotel from the reception, you go by the stairs and into the Baronial Hall. The hall dates from around 1500. An inscription reads:

"Iohn Dalston Elisabet mi wyf mad ys byldyng"

The letters are in Gothic script, and curiously written in reverse.

Above the Baronial Hall is a gallery. It's here the oldest ghost - known to the staff as Lady Jane, can be seen. She appears in Tudor dress and may well be one of the family actually called Dalston who owned the Hall for many decades.

Off the Baronial Hall to the left an old wooden doorway opens onto a staircase. Near the bottom of the stairs is a heavy iron gate which dates from the time the hall was first built. From what is today the back of the hotel, the two ancient towers are plain to see. This staircase spirals up worn stone steps to the top of the left tower.

The stairs come out in what's now the honeymoon suite complete with a four poster bed. The walls are the original stone and the windows cut through blocks three feet thick. This tower's even older than the Baronial Hall and dates from the early Middle Ages when it was a pele tower put up as a defence against the Scots.

The Honeymoon Suite isn't haunted but it's atmospheric enough despite that. If you climb past its door up the stairs, you emerge onto the battlements and from them you can get even higher to the top turret. From here you look south to the Lake District fells.

Going down again, on the ground floor there's a small library which serves as a lounge for residents. On the same corridor, there's also a cupboard for hanging coats. When the back panel of this cupboard was removed during renovation it revealed a staircase going up to meet a blank wall.

From this floor the staff can go down to the extensive

cellars that wind like a rabbit warren underneath the hotel and almost travel in time from modern plaster, Victorian bricks and medieval stone. There are storm drains down here and when the rain's heavy the cellars flood.

More than one of the porters have heard noises from the cellars when making their rounds in the depths of the night. It's been described as the sound of wooden barrels being manhandled and rolled around. But, wooden barrels have not been used for a long time at Dalston Hall. In 1997, during the daytime the noises were heard and one brave fellow called Richard actually went down to investigate. He said he saw the figure of a man, but losing his nerve, he turned and came back up again. He asked the receptionist who the other fellow was. The receptionist told him that he must be mistaken; there was definitely no one else down there.

After I had interviewed the staff at Dalston Hall, I came across another account of the ghost in the cellar in Liz Linahan's book, *The North of England Ghost Trail*. She refers to a workman renovating the Hall in the 1960s who met a man in the cellar who helped him by handing him tools. Needless to say the man vanished. Richard wasn't aware that his ghost in the cellar had been reported so many years before.

Room 4 is said to be haunted by a poor maid who threw herself from the pele tower above. It has an original fireplace with inglenooks to either side. A female member of staff, Lisa Avey, and her partner stayed there one night but both had difficulty getting to sleep. She told me that she had a strong feeling of a presence in the right hand inglenook - as if someone were watching them both while they slept.

One guest came down in the morning and asked to be moved from Room 4. She said she woke up to hear her dog growling at the door. It kept growling on and off all night, though there was no one to be seen. She said she herself had begun to feel a presence in the room.

In 1996 another guest awoke to find a lady sitting on the bed next to him. She spoke to him but her voice came from somewhere behind him, not from her mouth. He couldn't afterwards remember a word she'd said, but hadn't been frightened at all during the experience.

There are also sounds of things being dragged over wooden floorboards in the night. Yet, these days there are no wooden floorboards - all the floors are carpeted.

Room 12 is perhaps the most interesting; it has half a bathroom. It's difficult to see from inside, but if you go outside the Hall and look into the bathroom window, you'll see that the room has been cut in half and divided with a false wall. Though the faded decor of the closed off half is visible from outside, there's no way to get to it without knocking a hole in the wall.

Room 12 has a lovely view of the gardens, perhaps the best view of any room in the hotel. It also has a four poster bed. People who have slept in the room - not everyone but a significant number over the years - have complained of being woken by girls' voices whispering. No one has said anything untoward happened, they sound as if they are just having a giggly time. The trouble is - there's nobody actually there.

Liz Linahan reports that in October 1996, the candles used for the medieval banquets held in the Baronial Hall were seen by staff to flare up by themselves. During the same month, glasses were heard to smash in empty rooms, and were found broken a good distance from the shelf they had been stacked on; pint glasses rose into the air on their own; the library windows were discovered flung open and the night porter reported the sound of planks banging together.

In October 1997 the telephone system went haywire and all the phones began to ring at once. When they were answered, there was no one there, yet they kept ringing every ten minutes until they stopped as mysteriously as they'd begun. Lights also flickered on and off and the fire alarm system reported fires that had not occurred.

Leave Dalston Hall and turn left out of the drive. Go through the village of Dalston and look out for a left turn for the M6 and Durdar. When you come to the roundabout over the M6 take the third exit off it for Wetheral. Just as you enter Wetheral take the minor country lane to your right (it's the second right after Cumwhinton). This bends left and you'll see the remains of the priory to your right. You can park in the Priory car park.

Wetheral and Great Corby

Wetheral priory was founded when Cumbria was under Scottish rule. It's quite a pretty village which is now a commuter base for people working in Carlisle. If you walk left out of Priory Gatehouse and down the lane, you'll see a public footpath going across a field to your left. This leads to woods above the River Eden.

The woods are pleasant, particularly in Spring and Summer. If you follow the path along the cliff top you'll see another path descending steeply to your left towards the river which becomes sandstone steps cut into the rock. They can be a slippery so be careful if you chose to go down. They lead down to St Constantine's Cells.

St Constantine was of the royal house of Strathclyde and Cumbria, but it was a common name so exactly which Constantine he was is difficult to say. His cells are cut into sandstone. On the wall on your right, before you get to the cave proper, you'll see a quotation in Welsh. It was put there by a 19th Century antiquarian, but it was composed in the 6th Century, when the Welsh and Cumbrian languages were the same, by Llywarch the Old - also of the royal house of Cumbria (descended, by the way, from Old King Cole). It laments the briefness of life -

This leaf, persecuted by the wind
Already old, though born this year.

From the top of the path you can look over the river and on the other bank you'll see a statue of St Constantine. This is actually in the grounds of Corby Castle. Corby Castle isn't open to the casual wanderer, so you'll have to look at it from this side of the river.

Corby Castle has been owned by the Howards since 1611 and has a very famous ghost. This story has been told many times, but the ghost is so unusual that it's worth repeating. The ghost is known as 'The Radiant Boy', he appears from nowhere and is full of a golden light. He's said to smile gently and be completely unthreatening. Those who see him are destined to have great power but unfortunately come to a violent end.

A number of the Howards have seen the Radiant Boy. One of them, Lord Castlereagh, became Foreign Secretary of Great Britain in the great days of Empire, then in 1822, cut his throat when the balance of his mind was disturbed. A local clergyman from Greystoke also saw the Radiant Boy in 1803. He was lying awake in the dark next to his wife when he saw a glimmer in the room which grew to a bright flame. He thought something had caught fire, but to his amazement he beheld a beautiful boy, clothed in white with golden hair. He had a mild and benevolent expression, stayed for a while and then glided towards the fireplace and disappeared through the wall.

The clergyman lived to be an old man, though not particularly famous, and died in his bed.

A more recent sight of the Radiant Boy was in 1965 when a local postman was cycling to work a while before dawn on a dark winter morning. He looked up at Corby Castle from the road and saw a golden light around the battlements. At first he thought it was the sun rising, but it was too early and besides the castle was to the west of him. He was rather puzzled so he got off his bike and stopped for a while to look. Then he saw the Radiant Boy above the battlements. After that the postman disappeared from history and probably lived to a ripe old age.

From Wetheral, you can walk over the railway bridge into Great Corby, or just go down to the river where the ferry used to go from and enjoy the pleasant surroundings. Great Corby itself is another pleasant village. There's a pub there called the Queens Inn and a strange red sandstone structure which looks like a folly, but was built in 1833 as a blacksmith's shop.

Brampton

Leave Wetheral. Follow the road through the village; it eventually comes to a junction with the busy A69 just by a bridge over the Eden. Turn right over this bridge and continue in the direction of Newcastle. You'll come to a roundabout. Take the exit off the main A69 and go into the market town of Brampton.

Brampton has a lot of history - Bonny Prince Charlie stayed here while his troops laid siege to Carlisle. As you come into the town, you'll see a monument on your right to the Capon Tree. This was the place where six Jacobite rebels were hanged in 1745 and they're still supposed to be seen on the anniversary of their execution dangling at the end of ghostly ropes. The Capon Tree was an ancient oak and the story is that judges travelling between the courts at Carlisle and Newcastle would stop at this spot to feast on fat capons and enjoy the shade of the tree.

If you're low on petrol, you should fill up in Brampton, because there are no petrol stations on the itinerary until we get back to Carlisle.

Go through Brampton and take the left turn from, the green that points in the direction of Lanercost.

Lanercost

There aren't many houses at Lanercost, but once upon a time it was the site of the most important Priory in this part of Cumbria. It was founded about 1166 by the Augustinian Canons.

In this rural area, close to the Roman Wall and dominated by a ruined monastery, there remained, until very recently, a belief in elves. The fair folk were thought to be around and about quite often and one of the local clan was Morgana La Fée, the lady who tended King Arthur as he lay dying and took him off to Avalon. In 1900 a local man said he'd found tiny tobacco pipes which he claimed belonged to fairies.

The Abbey Bridge Inn at Lanercost is an atmospheric place which has been, tastefully modernised. As the name suggests it's by the ancient bridge over the River Irthing and close by Lanercost Priory. The Abbey Bridge Inn is a pub, but in a separate building there are rooms for guests. No one has ever seen a ghost in any of the rooms, as far as I know, but there are stories that lights go on and off and electrical equipment behaves strangely. These things are associated with ghostly activity in many other places. With the ruined priory so close and the tales of elves in the woods, there surely should be something to think about as you lie in bed in Lanercost, deep in the countryside, folded amongst the hills and woods.

Birdoswald

Near to Lanercost is Hadrian's Wall. The first sight of the Wall - still recognisably a Wall after all these centuries - is very impressive. Hadrian's wall was built on the northern frontier of the Roman Empire in about 120 and today its remains are a World Heritage Site. Birdoswald was one of the many forts along and there's a first rate visitors' centre there today.

Continue on through Lanercost, past the Priory and up the narrow road that runs beside the remains of the Roman Wall. After passing the ruins of a mile turret, you see Birdoswald on your right.

The reason that this site is included in this book is that in Roman times it was called Camboglanna and possibly connected with legends of King Arthur. Camboglanna could well be Camlann the site of Arthur's last battle where he was treacherously murdered.

North Cumbria's full of stories that recall the adventures of the Once and Future King. Some people have it that the dying Arthur was carried along the Roman road from here to the sea and then put in a ship to Ravenglass, once known as Aveling - perhaps the real Avalon? More of Ravenglass later.

If you continue on past Birdoswald and turn left onto the B6318 you'll pass a farm on your left with a ruined medieval tower next to it. This is Triermain which also has an Arthurian story attached to it. This story was retold by Sir Walter Scott in *The Bridal of Triermain* and concerns the marriage of King Arthur's daughter giving as her dowry:

Both fair Strath-Clyde and Reged wide,
And Carlisle town and tower.

Bewcastle

From Triermain head west along the B6318 past signs for the strangely named Desoglin and Tercrosset. After you pass a house called Longlands on the left you come to a cross-roads. Turn right for Bewcastle. This area has a remote and uninhabited feel to it. These hills are often haunted by mists and dark shapes loom up, metamorphosing into trees or cows as you get closer.

Bewcastle lies in what most people would feel was the middle of nowhere, but it's all the better for that. It consists of a small stream - the Kirk Beck, a pub, a church, a farmhouse and ruined castle.

The church and castle sit on a small plateau. There's an exhibition of the church's history in a building in the churchyard. You'll also pass a remarkable monument - an Anglian cross that's lost its head.

The earliest parts of the church date from 1200, but the cross is from about 670. There's an inscription on it in Anglo Saxon runes which commemorate Alcfrith son of Oswi, once king of Northumbria. The carving is quite exquisite and dates from the high tide of Northumbrian culture and power. The carving's wholly Christian and shows links to Mediterranean sculpture - some of the carvings are of vine leaves which even then didn't grow in this cold part of the world.

The castle, now in ruins, was founded in 1092 probably by William Rufus - the son of the Norman Conqueror, who obtained Cumbria from Scotland. He gave the castle to a certain Bueth, but then Bueth's grandson Robert actually fought for the Scots against the English. However by 1565 we know the castle was in a bad state of repair and it has stayed that way.

Both the castle and the church are built partly of masonry from the Roman fort underneath them. You can still see the ditches and hummocks in the ground which mark the Roman fort. It was built to police the area to the north of the Roman Wall. Within the Roman fort were found solid silver plaques given as offerings to the Celtic god Cocidius who was a god of soldiers. These are now on display in Tullie House museum in Carlisle. In the western parts of the Wall area, Cocidius seems to be equated with Mars, the Roman god of War. His name could mean something like the 'red one'. There's an Irish god known as Dá Choc who may be another form of Cocidius.

This area from Bewcastle south to the valley of the River Irthing was the cult centre of this warrior god. An interesting relief of the Mother Goddess sitting in a chair with fruits in her lap was also found at the fort at Bewcastle. The mother goddess was handed down in tradition as Modron, and her son was Mabon - the great son. Mabon - or Maponos as an earlier form, had his cult centre at Lochmaben, just over the border in Scotland.

It's interesting that the invading Northumbrians chose Bewcastle as the place to set up an important Christian monument, but this often happened at old pagan sites.

As you would expect with all these gods and goddesses in such a remote spot, the local pub, the Lime Kiln, and the smithy cottage behind it are haunted. One of the figures seen around the pub is a Roman Centurion.

Near Bewcastle on the banks of the White Lyne it's told that a local man coming home from the pub was grabbed and pulled off his horse by fairies. They were about to drag him into an entrance to the underworld in the side of a hill but he pulled out a Bible and they fled.

Catlowdy and Kershope Forest

From Bewcastle follow the road west until you join the B6318 again. Turn right here towards Sleetbeck.

Near Sleetbeck is a place called Friars Hill and at a house in this spot a man delivering coal saw a monk walk through a wall. There was also a sinister white shape like a sheet seen flapping around on the roads thereabouts by one or two people at various times. This may remind you of the frightening ghost story by M R James *Oh, Whistle and I'll Come to You, My Lad*

You pass near the hill called Arthur Seat, though you can't see much of it because of the forestry plantation. Once again, note the Arthurian connection. Go through the hamlet of Catlowdy. Continue along that road but when you come to the Bridge Inn, turn left. If you continue straight on you're over the Liddel Water and into Scotland.

Continue on the road through the straggling houses that make up the hamlet of Carwinley, and then down to Longtown. Carwinley was once the 'caer' or fortress of Gwenddolau.

Go into Longtown and turn left onto the main road. Take the first right onto the minor road past Fauld Mill to Arthuret church. A panel has been set up to commemorate the battle of Arthuret in the parking bay on the other side of the road from the church. Gwenddolau fought at this battle which took place in 573. No one knows what the dispute was about though record that it was over 'a lark's nest' - perhaps the nearby site of Caerlaverock castle which guards the Solway Firth and could mean the 'fort of

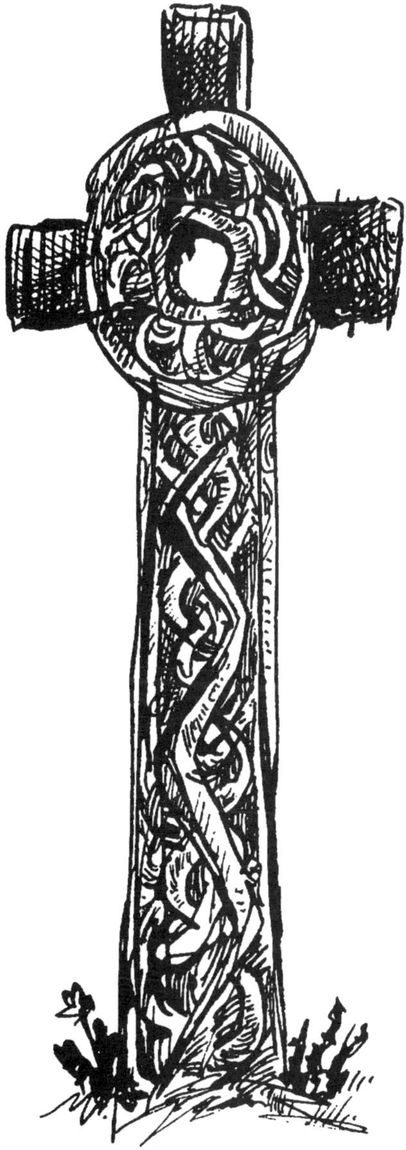

the lark'.

Gwenddolau's court bard (or druid, because there's some suggestion that he was still a pagan) was Myrddin, better known as Merlin. Whatever the cause, Gwenddolau was fighting his cousins, fellow descendants of Old King Cole, and he lost. Gwenddolau was killed and Merlin went mad and wandered in the great forests of Scotland where he had some strange conversations with a little pig, as recorded in the Black Book of Carmarthen.

The Welsh triads record the battle of Arthuret as one of the three futile battles of the Island of Britain. The other two were Camlann (perhaps at nearby Birdoswald) at which Arthur was slain and the strange Battle of the Trees (Cad Goddeu).

The Church at Arthuret has an ancient preaching cross in the graveyard with lozenge designs on it which W G Collingwood said was Norman in origin. To the west of the church, more than half overgrown is a holy well dedicated to St Michael. St Michael is of course the great Archangel who fights the enemies of god, and a dedication to him often signifies that the church was built on a site of an earlier pagan temple.

Carlisle

Carlisle, the great border city - was once the site of the Roman fort of Luguvallium - named after someone full of the power of the great god Lugos. Dedications to various Celtic gods have been found inside the city walls, including the Horned God and the Great Mother.

Carlisle has long been a border city; it was fought over between English and Scots for centuries. St Cuthbert visited in Anglo Saxon times as was shown a working Roman fountain, centuries after the Romans had left. It was the capital of the great Urien Rheged, whose son, Owain and his magical flock of ravens we have already mentioned. Disentangling history from legend is always difficult, but it's possible that Carlisle is the only city in Britain - including London - to be continuously inhabited from Roman times to the present day.

Local legend has it that underneath the city is a network of tunnels. These mysterious tunnels are supposed to be haunted and there's a ghost who travels from the Cathedral to the Friar's Tavern in Devonshire Street. It's said the residents of the old part of the city hear mysterious knocking sounds from below the ground. Whenever a new building's put up in this area, the archaeologists are always keen to do a dig, because of the denseness of history under the streets.

A lot of stories of Carlisle's ghosts were collected by Gerald Findler in his *Ghosts of the Lake Counties*. Near the railway station are the Citadel Towers. These are fakes - rebuilt versions of those erected at the command of Henry VIII. A grey lady can be seen wandering around here at odd times.

Around the Cathedral is a network of old cobbled streets. It's recorded that in 1868 a number of people saw a midget dressed in old fashioned clothes with silver buckles on his shoes and wearing knickerbockers. Though he seemed quite happy, there was something odd about him because he vanished into thin air.

Mr Findler also records the Citadel Bar ghost. Before this pub, still there today, was modernised in 1967 a number of people saw a man come in, order a bottle of beer and then disappear through a brick wall, leaving his drink behind. The incident was recorded in the local paper years later in 1976, where witnesses said the ghost was wearing 17th Century clothes.

In *Ghosts & Legends of the Lake District* by J A Brooks, he records the ghost of a cavalier seen by the city's western walls, often early in the morning.

I was told a story by a Scotsman who'd come to live in Carlisle in 1959 to work as a jeweller. He and a partner started business in a former bank near Victoria Viaduct. There were a number of people working in the building which was narrow and tall with a long staircase going up from the cellar to the topmost floors. The building had small windows and was very dark. It wasn't too long before people working late heard footsteps climbing the stairs when they thought they were alone. If they looked out they saw no one. This went on for some months and soon people would refuse to work after dark, or if they had to, they'd leave in a rush, taking the stairs two at a time to get out. They said the stairs had an odd atmosphere after dark, although during daylight they were fine. Things started to be moved around overnight. One day, when they tried to get into the cellar they found the huge iron door, from when the cellar was a bank vault, had been taken off and lodged against the door from inside. It took a whole gang of men to shift it out of the way.

One particular night they tried to trap whoever was climbing the stairs. It was such a tall building that they had an intercom system from one floor to another. One of the workers stationed in the lower floors heard the footsteps go up the stairs. He used the intercom to tell those waiting and then they all rushed out. There were no doors that anyone climbing the stairs could have darted into but there was nobody to be seen.

A little later when building work was being done, the heavy flagstones in the cellar were removed and underneath was found an old well. It was partially filled by rubbish, but to make it safe the builders wanted to pull the rubbish out and cap it properly. As they removed the accumulated debris, they found the skeleton of a man, upside down. When they pulled it out, they found that it had no head. It turned out that the skeleton was of considerable age and it was taken to the museum at Tullie House. After that time, the ghostly steps were heard no more.

One of the most impressive buildings in Carlisle is the Cathedral. This has an interesting history and fascinating architecture. It also has a bit of graffiti in Norse scratched in runes dating from the 13th Century.

There's a little pamphlet by a lady called Thirlie Grundy and is called *The Green Man of Carlisle Cathedral*. In it she talks about the sculptures of the medieval green man - a pagan rather than a Christian figure. They adorn many of the capitals of the pillars along the nave. Ms Grundy claims that this series of pagan carvings was to celebrate the breathing life of the natural world. Interestingly the green men always turn away from the altar and other foci of Christian worship. Ms Grundie argues that this, and green men at other medieval cathedrals were the product of a brotherhood of pagan stone masons who were given freedom to carve what they liked high up in the gloomy roof of the cathedrals.

Carlisle has a castle, which though originally founded by the Normans, continues in daily use. As might be expected, there are a few ghost stories connected with it. there's the spirit of a woman who has been seen many times. She so frightened one guard in 1823 when the castle was occupied by the military that he bayoneted the figure. He struck so hard that his bayonet was embedded in the wall behind the ghost. He fainted and then died of shock the next day. Strangely the remains of a woman dressed in a tartan robe with gold rings on her fingers was found bricked into the wall of the upper keep.

In the early 1800s the cemeteries of Britain were plagued by the 'Resurrection Men' or body snatchers, who stole newly buried corpses and sold them to doctors for medical research.

In September 1823 a coach heading from Scotland to Liverpool had an accident just outside Carlisle. A boy aged six suffered a severely broken leg and it had to be amputated. Unfortunately, infection got a hold and the poor boy died. He was buried in St Cuthbert's church which is just behind the main shops of English Street on the way out to the West Walls.

In the November of that year there was great uneasiness in Carlisle because there were stories that the

Resurrection Men were about their grisly trade in the city. When an investigation was made at Stanwix churchyard, it was found that a coffin had been tampered with but the body had been left because it was in too decomposed a state to be of any use to them. This discovery led the authorities to mount an investigation into all of the city's churchyards and this proved that many of the graves had been desecrated. The trail led to two strangers who had hired a room in an area known as Long Island - well away from the main centres of population at that time - and suited to their business.

At that time there was a firm in Carlisle which delivered parcels and suchlike to Edinburgh. It was ascertained that on 5th November a strong box, well tied and nailed down had been sent to a Lieutenant Todd in Edinburgh. The box was intercepted at Hawick and when it was opened was found to contain the remains of three children.

The couriers at Carlisle remembered the man who had left the box because he had a strange face. Sure enough, some days later he came with another box, also nailed and tied. They refused to accept it.

On 8th December during a funeral service at St Cuthbert's a body was discovered half dragged out of its grave. It belonged to a local butcher buried the previous month. When the graveyard was carefully investigated it transpired that two other bodies had been removed, including that of the child killed as a result of the coaching accident.

The next day, a group of armed men went round to the place in Long Island that the two strangers had rented. They found that the two had fled. A woman nearby said she'd seen a man carrying a heavy package walking past her house in the early hours, after that she'd seen a second man with a similar burden, then a third. This road led from St Cuthbert's Churchyard to Long Island.

The strangers got away and though a reward of twenty

guineas was offered, the grave robbers were never caught.

From the centre of Carlisle, go over the viaduct, past the Mormon church, turn left at the roundabout by the tall Victorian factory tower and you'll go past the crematorium. Continue on this road and you'll find yourself back in Dalston.

BACK OF SKIDDAW & THE SOLWAY COAST

Hotel: Overwater Hall

The Lady From the Lake

Tel. 01768 776566

Tariff (1999): B&B £42

Getting There:

Driving: Go to Junction 40 of the M6 and take the A66 in the direction of Keswick. Go past Keswick and watch out of Bassenthwaite Lake on your right. When you've left the lake behind, look out for a sign for Castle Inn pointing to the right. Take that turn. Follow the road until you see a hotel called Castle Inn on your left at a cross roads. Turn right then immediately left. Keep on that road until you see a right turn from which Overwater Hall's signposted. Overwater is down a drive through some trees on your right a little way down this road.

Public Transport: Public Transport isn't plentiful around Overwater. For advice telephone 01228 606000

There's no village of Overwater, only the small lake lurking in the shadow of the mountains. This part of the Lake District National Park is virtually unknown to visitors and has a very remote feel. In Autumn you'll see a spread of golden leaves on the lake; a little later in the year and the water's edge is fringed by jagged knives of ice but it will never freeze over.

Overwater Hall is a welcome sight on a cold day, though you aren't struck by its unexpectedly formal front until you turn into the courtyard. There are Doric columns and plaster busts in the portico. The house is proud with a

SILLOTH
SKINBURNE
BECKFOOT
WOLSTY
ALLONBY
ABBEY TOWN
MARYPORT
A596
WIGTON
DOVENBY
TALLENTIRE
BOTHEL
GREENHILL
BRIDEKIRK
A595
BLINDCRAKE
B5305
COCKERMOUTH
ISLE
A66
BEWALDETH
IREBY
B5299
OVERWATER HALL
BASSENTHWAITE LAKE
CALDBECK

castellated top and bowed front; out of place and yet still at home in this remote place. So different from the stone farmhouses around; it hasn't grown out of the landscape, it's been defiantly placed there. But at the same time the landscape has overpowered it and reclaimed it. Though it might want to be in Italy, or in Surrey, or some place far away, it will never escape these mountains. Neither will some of its inhabitants.

Overwater Hall was built shortly before 1811 by a certain Mr Gaff. It was then sold to a family called Gillbanks by at least 1814. Joseph Gillbanks was born in 1780 and sailed off to make his fortune in Jamaica. In the Eighteenth Century the ports of Cumberland, particularly Whitehaven, had strong trading links with the West Indies. Joseph set himself up as a merchant in Jamaica and, in due course, became wealthy and married the niece of the Chief Justice there. Whether he loved her or whether it was a marriage brought about in the interests of trade is hard to say; but legend has it that he started an affair with a poor black girl on the island.

In 1814 Joseph returned to Cumberland with his legal wife and bought Overwater Hall. He put any improprieties he may have been guilty of in Jamaica behind him and had the Gillbanks family motto *Honore et Virtute* emblazoned above the entrance, where it proudly sits to this day. Joseph became a magistrate and quickly took on the role of a respectable country gentleman.

But it wasn't long before his past came to haunt him. The young black girl, whose name isn't known, followed him all the way to England. Though he'd forgotten her, she couldn't forget him. Perhaps she loved him, perhaps she was pregnant; we'll never know, but it's easy to imagine the panic her appearance would have caused in the respectable Mr Joseph Gillbanks.

After she arrived, still pretending to love her, Gillbanks took her out on Overwater Tarn in a rowing boat. Talking of this and that, he rowed her to the middle of the lake.

Finally, she suspected something was amiss and tried to make him take her to land. Gillbanks grabbed at her and pushed her overboard. Overwater's a remote stretch of water even today, in those days is seems unlikely anyone would have heard her screams. She tried to climb back into the boat but Gillbanks had come prepared for murder. He took out a concealed sword and chopped off her arms as she clung to the boat.

Gillbanks then continued his career as a Magistrate and on his death at the age of 73 received a glowing obituary in the Carlisle newspaper of the day.

After that, Gillbanks disappears into history, but not so the unfortunate black girl. Ever since - right up to a few months ago - guests and staff have reported seeing the apparition of a black girl with no arms and a bonnet like head-dress high up on her head.

Traditionally she appears at New Year, when a tapping is heard against one of the outside windows. At other times, voices are heard in corridors but when a search is made, no one can be found.

She particularly favours Room 3, (perhaps because this is the only room in the house from which the Tarn can be seen) and has been seen walking through the door there. One night a lady sleeping with her husband in that room woke to find a glowing apparition wearing a head-dress near her bed. She shook her husband but couldn't manage to wake him. She lay there terrified until the spirit vanished.

One lady has been a regular guest at Overwater for some time. One night she was booked into Room 3. The next morning she said though she would be pleased to come back to Overwater, she never wanted to stay in Room 3 again. She gave no reason, but the staff made their own assumptions.

Early in 1998, an AA inspector came to do an inspection to make sure the hotel was up to scratch. His name was Mr Charlton and he stayed in Room 3. The owner of Overwater

told me that Mr Charlton had come down the next day and told him of a strange experience that he'd had in the room. I telephoned Mr Charlton at AA headquarters and at first he thought I wanted to talk about a ghostly experience he'd had in Brighton. I told him that it was actually Overwater Hall I was interested in. There was a long silence and then he said; "Overwater, near Bassenthwaite... I remember something happening there." There was another pause and then he said, "you know, all I can remember is talking very animatedly to the owner about it the next morning. I know something happened, but I can't remember what."

It was odd that he was obviously struggling to remember an event which should have been rather memorable. He said it felt weird. He knew that something remarkable happened, but it was as if there was some block on his memory. As we spoke, he suddenly he said, "I remember a light in the room. I don't know where it came from. That's all."

We finished the conversation. He was definitely doing his best to remember what had happened to him, and he was baffled that somehow it seemed to have been wiped from his memory.

I mentioned that Overwater Tarn never freezes over. This is because, even in the coldest weather, a severed black hand pushes through the ice and breaks it open. Even in death, the poor black girl will not surrender to her fate and be sealed in the cold dark waters of the lake.

The black lady isn't the only ghost at Overwater. For many years a grey terrier dog was often seen inside the house. The hotel accepts guests' dogs, so most other guests assume it belongs to someone else. Only the staff know the dog is seen time after time with no apparent owner. The dog hasn't been seen for a little while, but the mystery of who it might be was stumbled on by the hotel's proprietor, Stephen Bore, after he went for a walk in the grounds.

Past the ruined ice house, hung with moss and ivy, and through the curtains of overhanging willows, a short walk through beds of briars and nettles, redolent with the smell of wild garlic and damp earth, will take you to a half overgrown gravestone. It's small and the inscription shows it to mark the resting place of two little dogs. It reads:

"Lyulph - Sec a bonnie dog - 1892 - 1906
Brownie - Too Dearly Loved - 1899 - 1906

Binsey

To the west of Overwater, there's a mountain called Binsey Fell. There's a very strange story about a man who lived in a village nearby, possibly High Ireby. He was such a wicked man that local people said he was the devil. One night he was visited by an angel which gave him a warning: unless he did something to atone, he would go to hell and burn in eternity. The only way he could show he'd mended his ways was to build a church from top to bottom between sunset and sunrise.

The man was so frightened that he started to build straight away, carrying the stones in his leather apron. However sunrise came upon him too soon, and in his fright his apron fell open and the stones fell out, forming Binsey Fell. The fell has many large boulders and Bronze Age cairns on the top, which might have given rise to the story.

However stories of the devil carrying aprons of stones are common - though he usually builds bridges: see the section on Kirkby Lonsdale. However, if you're around Binsey on a misty night you may well see the silhouette of a man carrying stones.

To Caldbeck

From the drive of Overwater Hall turn right. Go on for a little while with the tarn on your right. Take the first right, the next left and keep on this road till the T-junction on the moor. Turn right and if you keep on this road and follow the signs you'll come to Caldbeck

The church at Caldbeck is dedicated to St Kentigern, otherwise known by his pet name of Mungo. St Mungo is the patron saint of Glasgow, which was the capital of the medieval kingdom of Strathclyde and Cumbria. St Mungo preached in this part of Cumbria on his way south to meet St David in Wales. Despite this saintly attention, Caldbeck has rather more than its fair share of ghosts.

One of the houses in the village is called Bushay House. There's a light seen there in the garden around midnight. A little distance away, the Rectory has a room to the front of the house which is haunted by a ghost which rattles chains but is never seen.

In the lanes around Branthwaite near Caldbeck, there's a huge black dog which appears near a holly tree. It will rush along the road for a while before suddenly disappearing. It can be seen at night around the village, but beware, because to see it traditionally portends a death.

The Priests Mill at Caldbeck isn't haunted as far as I know, but it's been nicely restored as a tea room. There's also a jeweller and a second hand book shop. Behind the Mill, a rickety bridge gives good views down to the River Caldew - the cold river itself.

From the small car park in front of the Priest's Mill, walk along the beckside behind the church. You'll come to a bridge and on the west side of the bridge is a holy well, dedicated to St Mungo. It reputedly has healing powers.

In St Kentigern's Churchyard is the grave of the famous hunter John Peel. The song *D'ye ken John Peel?* was written in a house near the Oddfellows Arms.

Walk through Caldbeck, past the Oddfellows Arms and out on the road back to Overwater. After about fifty yards you come to a stone barn on the right hand side of the road. Go through the wooden gates, through the wood and you'll come to an area known as the Howk. There's a ruined mill here, but the main interest is the gorge with the waterfall and the eroded recesses in the rock. This is Fairykirk - the fairies' church. You may be lucky enough to see one.

The Oddfellows' Arms

Tel. 01697 478227

Tariff (1999) : £25 B&B

Caldbeck has only one pub - The Oddfellows Arms. This pub is most definitely haunted. It has some rooms for accommodation and more are being refurbished. The Oddfellows Arms is owned by Jennings Brewery but before it was taken over by the Jennings, it was owned by one family for a long time. They had an elderly live-in aunt who died upstairs in the pub. It's her that gets the blame for the strange goings on.

There have been many ghostly occurrences at the Oddfellows and a presence is sensed throughout the building. In the kitchen, sauce bottles have flown out several feet from a shelf to crash to the floor and break. Upstairs in the manager's flat the ghost is often felt and moves the curtains on nights of dead calm.

When she's seen, the ghost is a woman in a brown dress. She can appear at any time of the year, but most often makes herself known during the winter from September to March.

Her most upsetting manifestations are on winter nights when the barmaids come into the dark bar to get everything ready. They often switch on the lights to find a woman in brown standing next to them. Invariably they run out of the bar shrieking and vow never to go in again. When they do go back, she's always gone.

To Wigton

The road forks on either side of the Oddfellows Arms, take the right hand fork and head in the direction of Carlisle.

After half a mile or so, you come to a crossroads. Continue straight over along the B5299 towards Wigton. You come out eventually to a junction with the main Cockermouth to Carlisle road, the A595. If you turn left and travel on the road for a short while, you'll see a mansion called Greenhill Hotel. You can stay there, take a drink or have a meal. It's also haunted

Greenhill Hotel

Tel. 01697 343304

Tariff (1999): £50

The Greenhill Hotel was built as a grand country house and is now a hotel. Even in the 19th Century it had the reputation of being haunted; the ghost there would extinguish the lights on carriages and bicycles.

Nowadays, the local Rotary Club meets at the Greenhill Hotel and when I was researching this book, I heard that more than one of them had seen an apparition in broad daylight, and this had happened on more than one occasion. However, no one would talk to me about it. From their reaction, they were obviously quite startled by what they had seen. Someone else in Wigton told me that the ghost is well known in the town. It's the spirit of a maid who hung herself in the cellar.

Though there may be no connection, in 1965, a sculpted head in the local red sandstone was found in the wall of the farm on the other side of the road from the Greenhill Hotel. It was dated from the Celtic period with typical huge eyes and lack of a mouth. Sculpted heads are found all over the Celtic world and the Romans knew the Celts as head hunters to whom the human head had a mystical significance. In southern France, Celtic sacred groves have been found with huge collections of skulls in them. In the north of England at the tribal hill fort of the Brigantes, archaeology shows us that skulls were stuck on top of the gate posts at the fort's main entrance.

Wigton

Wigton has the reputation of being the most haunted town in Cumbria. In *Ghosts & Legends of the Lake District*, J A Brooks gives an impressive list: The Church Street Phantom, the Clinic Ghost, the Burnfoot Spirit, the Water Street Boggle, the New Street Headless Horror and others.

He also talks about the Crown & Mitre's suicide room. The room has long been sealed up but strange noises still come from it. One night the daughter of the then landlord went to sleep in that room. She woke up in the middle of the night and, in the dark, stretched out for her candle. Instead she touched a cold and clammy human face.

Mr Brooks also mentions the Kildare Court Boggle. The current Kildare Hotel was once the Conservative Club. When it was being built in the 1880s the boggle appeared. An eye witness at the time reported that the boggle always appeared before a disaster. It was true in this case, one of the builders fell from a block and tackle he was riding on and was killed.

The current owner is a local man who took over the hotel in 1996. Since that time he and his staff have been nudged in the kidneys by a mischievous creature which, for a ghost, seems to be able to deliver solid digs in the back. Though this boggle is invisible, another ghost has been seen.

Around Christmas 1997, one customer saw a figure of a stoop backed old man smoking an old fashioned clay pipe climbing the stairs. He was surrounded by a hazy glow and the customer knew straight away he was a ghost .

One of the bar staff went down to change a barrel in the cellar and opened the door to see an old man sitting on the barrel. The owner has never seen the old man, but he says he has a strong feeling that someone's watching when he's down working in the cellar.

Round the corner is The Victoria. Its currently run by a

Mrs Taylor. One night towards the end of 1997, her boyfriend and a friend of his were up in the bar chatting. It was about half past one in the morning. They were talking about nothing much; the football scores, the weather. Then suddenly it was as if they were transported out of their own time. This lasted for about ten or twenty seconds, though it was difficult to say exactly how long because time seemed to run differently. They saw a group of people were walking and talking amongst themselves in the corner of the room. They were dressed in top hats and the women in shawls; something like the dress of the middle 1800s. What was strange however was that they were walking as if they were outside, going along a street, not inside the bar at all. They vanished as suddenly as they'd come. The two men looked at each other. They didn't know what to say, but they'd both seen the same thing.

The man I spoke to thought there was something about them that reminded him of show people. In the middle 1800s, before the pub was renamed the Victoria (previously it had been the Leg of Mutton) that corner of the bar wasn't there; it was part of the street. In those days when travelling show people came to Wigton, they'd stay in the alley behind the Leg of Mutton.

The only other report of strange goings on at The Victoria relate to the daughter of the house hearing laughter when there was no one around but her.

From the middle of Wigton, by the monument, turn left. At the junction, turn right onto the bypass and immediately left off it again. The signposts say Silloth. This is the B5302 and it runs straight to Abbey Town.

Abbeytown

The nave of the Abbey of Holme Cultram remains as the parish church of Abbey Town. It's much too big for the village since Henry VIII closed the monasteries and removed the Cistercian Monks in 1532. The Cistercians originally founded the abbey from the mother church at Melrose in 1150 when Cumbria was part of Scotland.

Cumbria later reverted to English ownership. Robert the Bruce's father was buried at Abbeytown but it didn't stop him burning Holme Cultram Abbey after the English lost the battle of Bannockburn in 1314.

Despite the history, the monks, and the wonderful piles of medieval stonework around the front of the Abbey, there are no ghosts.

Follow the signs for Silloth, and just when you're about to enter Silloth, look out for a sign to your right for Skinburness.

Skinburness

Go down a tree flanked lane, and along roads that carry warnings of flooding by the tide. At Skinburness, near Silloth, we have arrived at the sea - the very edge of England. Over the waves with their white mares' tails is Scotland and all around us are marshes. The signs on the roads mean what they say: these small roads are often inundated.

The first thing to note about Skinburness is the name. It's a Norse name which means the "Haunted Headland". Scotland is really very close across the Solway here, though on a poor day with lots of rain, it may be difficult to appreciate this.

When eloping couples on their way to Gretna Green got to the Cumbrian coast, for a fee, the local boatmen would row them over. One dark stormy night a boat set out from Skinburness but was lost among the raging waves. On certain nights the screams can still be heard. However the Norse name's older than this and shows that the area was associated with spirits and phantoms much earlier.

There's nothing much at Skinburness now; a hotel, the marshes, lots of birds. But this was the site of a thriving market town until 1302 when a great storm came and swept it into the sea.

Behind the Skinburness Hotel the spit of land pushes out among mud and reeds. Lots of small creeks wind among the salt marshes which are full of wildfowl and wading birds. This is Grune Point. An author no less than J R R Tolkein thought Grune Point might have been the location of the Green Chapel, where Sir Gawain came to find the Green Knight and have his head cut off. That's all lost now beneath the waves, but if you're there when the sea mist wreathes the marsh, and the silence broken only by the lonely cry of the curlew, watch out for the Green Knight!

Wolsty

Though his chapel was at Grune Point, the Green Knight's castle may have been at Wolsty. Take the coast road from Skinburness south through Silloth and on in the direction of Allonby. The dunes are to the right of you and if the day's clear you'll have good views of Scotland once you leave the houses behind. Take the first left just before you get into the hamlet of Beckfoot and keep on this lane till you see Wolsty Hall on the right. In the field behind the Hall are the foundations of Wolsty Castle - though actually this isn't visible from the road.

Wolsty was built by the Abbot of Holme Cultram in about 1327. This was the height of the Scottish wars and as mentioned above the monks of Holme Cultram had already been burned out by the Scots. Wolsty Castle was built as a place of refuge - particularly for their books. As all who have read Umberto Eco's *The Name of the Rose* will know, medieval monks often had occult works among their manuscripts.

In 1610, William Camden, the historian, wrote that the monks of Holme Cultram had in their possession the grimoires of the wizard Michael Scot. He was buried at Holme Cultram in 1290 and was widely regarded as a necromancer.

Scot was obviously a gifted scholar and mathematician

whose career spanned the border from Cumbria to Northumberland and over into Scotland. Another writer called Satchells visited Wolsty in 1629 and saw one of Michael Scot's books 'hanging on an iron pin in the castle.' He said no one dared to read it because they were terrified by Scot's reputation.

In 1654 Wolsty Castle was pulled down. Records of that time show that one of the rooms was known as Michael Scot's chamber. There are many stories about Scot: that, with the aid of demons, he could command the sea; that he built Bolton Old Church in one night; and that he and the devil between them built the mountain known as Criffel, which is the most prominent hill seen over the Solway on the Scottish side.

To Maryport

Return to the coast road and turn left, heading south in the direction of Allonby. You come through the hamlet of Beckfoot. Recently, three Roman cremation urns were washed out of a sandbank here and even after two thousand years they contained recognisable ash and bone. All down this coast are the remains of Roman defences and at Beckfoot, in the Roman Fort, was found a red sandstone altar to a Celtic horned god. He has short horns and long curling hair, with a garment over his shoulders.

The coast here can look very bleak in winter. This is the Solway Firth which as you go further south joins the Irish Sea and this whole area of water was once the realm of the sea god - Mannanán Mac Lír in Irish Gaelic, or in Welsh - Manawyddan Fab Llyr. His father was the original King Lear.

You pass through the village of Allonby with its horses grazing on the green near the sea's edge and then on to Maryport.

Maryport

Maryport was an extremely important Roman port. More recently, it has suffered industrial decline and is still quite poor, but the town, and particularly the harbour, are undergoing a renaissance. The town you see today was planned by local landowners, the Senhouses, built in a grid pattern on cliff tops overlooking the Solway.

We are heading for the Senhouse Roman Museum next to the lumps and bumps of the field that contains the Roman fort. The museum is in an old battery, that once held guns for naval gunnery practise.

The Senhouse Museum is important for its collection of altars to Roman and Celtic gods.

The most interesting piece in the collection is the so called Serpent Stone. I'ts phallic in shape with a horned serpent on one side and on the other a man's head in relief - a typical Celtic face with a wedge shaped face and staring eyes. Serpents rear up and frame the face. Both the man and the serpent wear torcs. The torc is a twisted rope of metal - many have been found around the Celtic world, some of solid gold.

I mentioned that the Celts revered the severed head; the torc also appears to have a religious as well as an ornamental function. The horned god Cernunnos, the lord of the beasts, wears one in many pieces of sculpture. The Roman temples at Bath in southern England also show sculptures that link the severed head with writhing serpents, and this was obviously a theme well known in the native religion in those times. What it meant, we can only guess, but the snake - which sheds its skin - is a common symbol for reincarnation - a doctrine of the Druids.

Also at Maryport we have sculptures and dedications to Setlocenia, the goddess of long life and the warrior god Belatucadros, perhaps a version of the great god Belenus, after whom the whole island of Britain was once named and in whose honour the Beltane fires (the fires of Bel) were lit. Some of the strangest gods are the three hooded gods - the Cucullatii who are found throughout Celtic Britain. Because of the shrouded faces and their hoods they're thought to be gods of death.

Also in Maryport is an altar dedicated to Sol Invicta - the Unconquered Sun. Sol Invicta was a recognised Roman god, but there are examples of this figure with rays coming out of his head very much in the Celtic style. This may be the Celtic god Ogmios. Ogmios is known from Britain and Gaul and also from Ireland where he is called Oghma. Oghma is the father of writing and a god of great strength. His surname is 'grianainech' the sunlike one. If Ogmios was worshipped in Cumbria, as seems likely it just might be that the Radiant Boy of Corby Castle descends from him.

The strangest deity in the Maryport collection is the so called Shadow Man. This carving shows a long figure lacking in any features apart from a pair of eyes. Who it is supposed to be is unknown.

When you come out of the Museum, look down from the cliffs and enjoy the magnificent views over the Solway Firth to Scotland. If it's night, you might be fortunate enough to see one of the three ghost ships of the Solway. *The Rotterdam* was lost nearly one hundred and fifty years ago with all hands. She's seen only before a maritime disaster. It's reported that whatever the weather, even if the sea's dead calm, *The Rotterdam* pitches and rolls among heavy waves. Ghostly figures are seen on her deck and their pitiful cries carry to the shore.

Another smaller ship was deliberately wrecked on the Solway in the last century and she's supposed to be seen on dark nights as well.

The final ghost ship dates from the 18th Century when Whitehaven was a rich port, trading with America and the West Indies. *The Betsy Jane* was a slaver, and returning from the New World, laden with gold earned by taking cargo after cargo of wretched humanity from Africa to the Caribbean. She sank in a storm as she was nearing her home port. She's seen around Christmas time, the anniversary of her sinking. Perhaps her master's fated to sail his ghost ship for eternity as a punishment for the suffering he inflicted on the poor slaves in his hold.

Tallentire

Go back down the hill from the Senhouse Museum and when you come to the traffic lights by the park, go straight over for Cockermouth. When you come to the village of Dovenby with a long wall on the right hand side of the straight road, you'll see a sign for Tallentire off to the left. Take this road through the wood.

There's a clump of trees on this road called *T' Hessles*. If you're walking or riding a bicycle beware; a hand is known to have reached out from the wood and grabbed at people - including a local district nurse in the days before they had cars. She was knocked off her bike.

Tallentire is a small, pretty village. It has a hall, built around 1770, but this is hidden down a drive and screened by trees. However, there's a story that at a certain place on the ground outside the Hall a red fungus known as Ghost's Blood grows. No matter how many times it's cleaned away, it's always back the next day. The story goes that a young girl was murdered most horribly there and her decapitated ghost wanders nearby to this day. There's also a story of treasure in the tower, but the Hall has been converted into flats and the tower flat has recently changed hands, so the new owner might want to spend some time knocking for hollow walls.

There's a house called Green Bank at Tallentire. J A Brooks tells that a girl stayed there in 1951, sleeping on a camp bed. In the middle of the night the bed was shaken so violently that she got up and ran out. Later she learned that the room had once been used as a temporary morgue after a number of people in the village were killed in a local disaster.

You can get a drink in The Bush in town, which is an authentic country pub. Not very long ago it was like going into someone's front room, everyone looked up curiously to see you and wondered whether you were undercover policemen come to check licensing laws.

Bridekirk

Turn back on yourself and head back towards Cockermouth. Just outside Tallentire you'll see a signpost to your left for Bridekirk. There's an interesting church at Bridekirk, though the current church only dates from 1868, it's built on an earlier site.

Cumbria was heavily settled by Norsemen in the 10th Century; they didn't come from Norway directly. They came to Cumbria from Ireland and the Isle of Man. They brought many Irishmen with them and also the Irish Saint Brigid. Brigid is interesting because she's clearly a Celtic goddess taken up by the Christian church.

There's evidence that she was a triple goddess with aspects as healer, metalworker, and poetess. Her name comes from a root meaning 'The High One.' Before the Irish Celts came, Brigid was worshipped by a British Celtic tribe in what the North of England, known as the Brigantes, so in a sense the Irish settlers brought her home in her new guise as saint.

In the church there is an inscription written in Runes on the Norman font. The language is Middle English and really it's a piece of graffiti that says "Rikart made me and brought me here". Among the dragons and centaurs there's a picture of Rikart on the font working away with his hammer.

Blindcrake

From Bridekirk, go down through the village in the direction of Cockermouth. When you come to the main road, turn left and then right into the hamlet of Redmain. Go through Redmain until you get to the village of Blindcrake.

One lady staying in a house in this village before electric lighting, woke up in the night and lit a candle, intending to read her book. Suddenly, she heard the sounds of soft singing and beautiful music. There was a noise as if chairs were being moved in the room underneath her bedroom. She wasn't in the least disquieted, and in the morning she asked her host who had been making the lovely music. The woman replied that other guests had heard the singing; the house was built on the site of an old chapel where monks had prayed in the Middle Ages.

Isel

We are now on the way back to Overwater Hall. To get back to the hotel, go from Blindcrake to Isel. Isel has a spectacular hall which dates from the time of Henry VIII. The Hall's occasionally open to the public. Ring Cockermouth Tourist Information Centre on 01900 822634 for details. At the village church, dedicated to St Michael, the slayer of monsters, there's a remnant of a Viking Age sculpted cross with a swastika decoration - a traditional good luck symbol before the Nazis got hold of it.

From Isel, head out on the country roads to Bewaldeth. Above the village is Binsey Fell. Overwater's the other side of this. To get there, go straight over the main road into Bewaldeth and out the other side. These are small, steep lanes, but carry on for about three kilometres and when you get to the cross roads, turn right down the hill. If you turn left at the bottom of the hill, you'll shortly find yourself outside the drive to Overwater.

THE CENTRAL LAKES

Hotel: Dale Head Hall

The Park Boggle

Tel. 017687 72478

Tariff (1999): £32.50-£47.50 B&B

Getting There.

Driving: From Junction 40 of the M6, take the A66 in the direction of Keswick. Go along the road until you're close to the (bypassed) village of Threlkeld. You'll see a sign pointing to your left indicating Thirlmere down the B5322. Take this road until you come to the junction with the A591. Turn left in the direction of Windermere. Look out for the Thirlspot Inn on the left hand side of the road and then almost immediately take a right down the drive to Dale Head Hall.

Public Transport: Train to Penrith, bus to Keswick. Take the Windermere bus from Keswick, but best check times on 01228 606000

Dale Head Hall has one of the most magnificent and unspoiled settings in the whole of the Lake District. The short driveway takes you through the trees, but leaves you unprepared for the view over Thirlmere from the front garden.

Though historically a private house, Dale Head was for a long time the property of the Manchester Water Board which extended Thirlmere to create a reservoir for that city. In his *Ghosts & Legends of the Lake District*, J A Brooks devotes a whole chapter to happenings around Thirlmere and Dale Head is mentioned. Mr Brooks retells an account written by John Richardson, a local schoolmas-

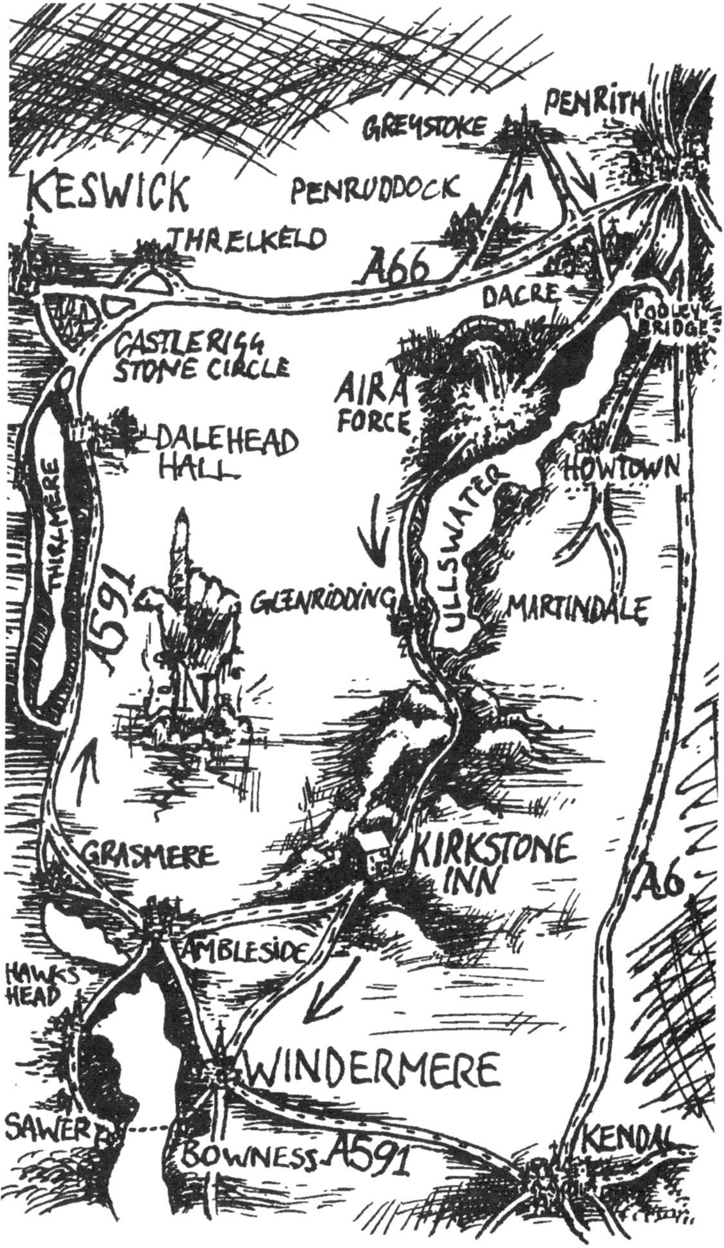
PENRITH
GREYSTOKE
KESWICK
PENRUDDOCK
THRELKELD
A66
DACRE
POOLEY BRIDGE
CASTLERIGG STONE CIRCLE
AIRA FORCE
DALEHEAD HALL
HOWTOWN
THIRLMERE
ULLSWATER
A591
GLENRIDDING
MARTINDALE
GRASMERE
KIRKSTONE INN
A6
AMBLESIDE
HAWKS HEAD
WINDERMERE
SAWER
BOWNESS
A591
KENDAL

ter and farmer in the middle years of the last century.

Richardson says that one night he was driving sheep back from their winter pasture when he got to Dale Head Park. It was dark when he arrived but he plodded on with the sheep and the dogs until, suddenly, the sheep stopped and became uneasy. Neither he nor the dogs could get them to go any further. In fact the dogs themselves got frightened and came to him, cowering against his legs. When he made his way to the front of the sheep to see what the problem was, he found a great mound of soil and stone. He had heard of the Park Boggle (the spirit that haunted that place) and thought it must be something to do with that creature. He spoke out loud, trying to reason with the boggle that he was only a poor farmer on his way home on a dark night.

Whatever he said did the trick because suddenly the sheep moved forward. When he got up to where the pile of soil had been, his foot encountered nothing at all. It seems that the boggle had taken on the form of the heap of earth as some kind of gentle mischief.

Richardson also saw the boggle another time. He was doing a bit of walling up on the fellside and by the time he was finished it had got dark. He was coming down into the valley when he saw a column of fire and sparks. Suddenly the light died away. More curious than frightened, he made his way over to where the fire had been but couldn't find any sign of burning. He took this to be the shape shifting boggle once again.

Dale Head Hall's drive is haunted because of a man who was murdered on his way home from the King's Head Inn. But it's the alleged murderer and not the victim who haunts the spot. After the crime occurred, the locals were so sure that a certain man locally had done it, that they turned against him and drove him out. He protested his innocence but was forced to flee. He went to Patterdale and lived the rest of his life in the caves there but after his death his spirit came back to the spot of the murder to

protest his innocence.

In 1995, new owners, Mrs and Mrs Lowe, moved into Dale Head Hall. Their daughter, Caroline, was sitting in the lounge on her own watching television. Her husband, Hans, was out and she was alone in the house. Quite unexpectedly she heard a loud noise from the ceiling. She describes it as a whoosh - like something heavy being dragged at speed from one side of the room to another. She says that it wasn't coming from the room above the lounge, it was actually in the lounge up by the ceiling; as if something invisible was making this enormous noise.

It started and stopped without a rumble or an echo and she admits to being very frightened. She said the room was filled with a strange presence as the noise started. She knew that the noise wasn't going to happen again, because the presence went.

Caroline heard other things in the old parts of the house after that. This ties in with what the previous owners reported; noises and feelings that someone's there with you. More than once guests have reported feelings of a presence, but no one has said it was unpleasant. In fact one sensitive lady said there were a number of spirits in the house, but they were all friendly

There are lots of original oak beams in the house. Much of it was added in the 1700s to an older core and you can still see the stone wall of the older house as an internal wall in the newer one. There's a very interesting feature in the older bedrooms; cupboard doors that open to reveal the mullioned Tudor windows; once they looked out to the surrounding hills, but now they only look at the walls encasing them.

The older parts of the house have uneven, bowed walls and floors which aren't straight. There's lots of dark wood everywhere and there's a charming stained glass window that's probably Victorian.

The only apparition that's been recorded is that of a young girl who visits guests in the old part of the house

(Rooms 6, 7 and 8)

In Room 7, as in the other older rooms, there are deep inglenooks at the side of the chimney breast. These were used for smoking ham or drying clothes. Room 7's tradition is that it was the cradle room and it's from these inglenooks the figure of a young girl comes out.

St John's in the Vale

Come out of Dale Head Park and turn left on the A591. If you arrived in the dark, you'll now be able to appreciate the beauty of this valley.

Though the mountains are very craggy, a particular outcrop on the right hand side of the valley is known as Castle Rock. This was the inspiration for Sir Walter Scott's tale of King Arthur called *The Bridal of Triermaine*. It's a favourite with climbers because it's so difficult, and it has a legend of having a boggle at the top of it. The belief that high and foreboding craggy heights have their guardian spirits or gods was certainly a common one in older times; consider Mount Olympus.

Look out for a right turn off the A591. It's signposted for Threlkeld. Take this and you'll be on the narrow road through the beautiful valley known as St John's in the Vale.

Castlerigg Stone Circle

After just over three kilometres, take the minor road off to the left. Take the left at the next T junction and you'll see signs for Castlerigg Stone Circle.

Castlerigg isn't the biggest stone circle in Britain, but with its crown of surrounding mountains, John Waterhouse in his book, *The Stone Circles of Cumbria*, called it 'one of the most visually impressive prehistoric monuments in Britain.' This is especially true in winter when the mountains are capped with snow. The circle is managed by the National Trust and gets a lot of visitors. Despite that, the scale of the setting makes it actually very difficult to crowd the place.

There were originally forty two stones but only thirty eight remain and the tallest is over two metres high. There's a rectangle of stones to the south east of the circle. But, though this was excavated in 1882, we don't know what it was used for and there's nothing like it at any other site in Britain. In 1854 we know there were three cairns in the middle. These were also excavated but the only things found within the circle were three stone age axes.

It's thought that Castlerigg is one of the earliest stone circles in Britain. Alexander Thom suggested that it was built as an astronomical observatory. The rising and settings of heavenly bodies were markers of important events in the agricultural year; the cycles of the sun, moon and stars almost always have ritual importance to the rhythms of life of tribal communities.

A line from one of the stones (no. 32 in Waterhouse's book) and the tallest stone lines up with the rising of the sun over High Rigg at Candlemass. In the opposite direction, it shows the position of the setting sun over Skiddaw during the summer solstice. The stones also point to significant lunar alignments.

There used to be an outlier to the east of the circle which pointed to the rising sun on May Day as it showed itself above Fiend's Fell in the Pennines. Waterhouse notes the coincidence that this lines up with a similar alignment from the stone circle called Long Meg in the Eden Valley east of here.

Return back on yourself until you see signs for Threlkeld. Follow these. The village of Threlkeld is just east of Keswick; signs point to roads into the village on the left hand side of the A66.

Threlkeld

Threlkeld, just off the A66, sits under glowering Blencathra whose name in early Cumbrian means *Devils' Peak*. Threlkeld's a small village but in 1671 was the scene of mass murder when a local man called Thomas Armstrong poisoned his wife, his three sisters-in-law, his father-in-law and the servant. He was hanged and suspended in gibbets near Windermere. He ghost was seen around there for many years.

A house called Threlkeld Place had the reputation of housing an indestructible guardian skull that was kept in a niche in the wall. When new owners moved in, it was taken out and buried with reverence. The next time the wife came to clean the room, she found the skull back in its place. They tried a couple more times to get rid of the skull, but it always came back. In the end, they bricked it in behind the niche where it remains today. More about skulls when we get to Windermere.

If you go back onto the A66 and head in the direction of Penrith, you'll soon leave Blencathra behind. The last shoulder of the mountain to your left is called Souther Fell. On Midsummer's Eve in 1735, two farm workers saw a ghost army marching , rank after rank, for over an hour over this fell. In 1745 many people saw the army again - also on Midsummer's Eve. As far as I know it hasn't been seen since.

Perhaps it was a memory of the Roman armies who once had their camps at Troutbeck. The ramparts can still be seen standing above the boggy ground in the valley by the side of the road just past Souther Fell.

Continue on through the bleak open landscape and look out for the conical hill known as Great Mell Fell to the right. Mell is the old Cumbrian word for a bald hill and the name has echoes of another cone shaped hill in north east Wales called Moel Famau: the Hill of the Mothers. Both perhaps refer to the sacred mother goddesses of the Celts.

Greystoke

Turn left when you see a sign for Penruddock. Continue on the road to Greystoke. Sadly Tarzan never lived here; he's made up.

You come to Greystoke after about 3 km along a narrow but fairly straight road. Greystoke is a well kept village with - rather bizarrely - an open air heated swimming pool. There's also a pub called *The Boot & Shoe*. You can stay there, and it's quite old, but I don't believe they have a ghost.

There is a ghost at Greystoke Castle however. Sadly, the castle isn't open to the public. The castle is the property of the Dukes of Norfolk who also own Corby and Naworth castles (both also haunted). There's a disused room in the tower at Greystoke that's haunted by a guest of a previous Duke of Norfolk. He'd been out hunting with the Duke and had gone to bed after a drinking bout but was never seen again. His clothes were found in his room but he himself had completely disappeared. Rumour has it that anyone staying in that room becomes very disturbed and cannot sleep.

There are also reports of mysterious knockings from inside the walls at Greystoke Castle and this apparently arises because there's a passage inside the walls haunted by the ghost of a monk who was deliberately walled in to die. This passage from the chapel to the bedroom where the man disappeared. It strikes me that it may not be a monk at all that haunts the passage, but the ghost of the man who found his way in but couldn't find his way out.

From Greystoke turn back on yourself onto the narrow road that leads to the A66. When you come to the A66, turn left towards Penrith, but get into the right hand lane of the dual carriageway as soon as you safely can. The turn for Dacre is on your right after only about a kilometre. Be careful of the traffic, and turn down the minor road to Dacre.

Dacre

Go along a country road with views to the fells in front. After about a kilometre and a half you'll find yourself in the village. Dacre's small but old - it was mentioned by the Venerable Bede in his writings and was the site of an Anglo Saxon monastery. There's one pub, which doesn't have accommodation.

Dacre Castle was built against Scottish raids in the Middle Ages, but it may stand on the foundations of a Dark Age fortress. The castle's now a private home with no public access, but this site is the traditional spot where three kings met to sign a peace treaty. In the castle there's a room called the Three Kings Room which is very haunted and an eerily cold wind whistles through it on nights of dead calm according to the grand-daughter of a maid who worked there at the beginning of the Twentieth Century.

The story does have a historical basis. In 927, Dacre, presumably because it was the closest monastery to the Cumbrian - English border at that time, was the site of a meeting between Athelstan of England, Constantine of Scotland and Owen of Cumbria. The peace didn't last and war broke out again in 937. However the affair must have been significant for the participants as their ghosts have lingered in Dacre ever since.

The most mysterious thing about Dacre is to be found in the churchyard. St Andrew's church is along a small, dead end lane that turns left off the main road just below the pub. If you go up there you'll see four ancient mysterious carved figures in the churchyard, generally known as the Dacre bears. They're said to be heraldic animals but why or when they were set up at the four corners of the church is unknown. Perhaps they're guardians? And perhaps they're older than the official medieval date, given the age of this site.

The number four is important. It's a protective number and, as any student of C G Jung will tell you, all good solid things come in fours. There are four points to the compass, four elements, four evangelists and four guardian bears at Dacre. And are they really bears? One of them has a lion's tail.

Go back to the main road, turn left and continue straight down until you come to the A592 and Ullswater. Turn left at the T junction and go to Pooley Bridge. You'll catch glimpses of the lake and its mountains through the trees, but the better views will come later. Then you can appreciate why it's considered one of the most beautiful of the lakes.

There's a hill fort on top of the wooded hill to your left as you enter the village.

To get to Martindale, either go along the narrow road along the east side of Ullswater, past the yachting club and the world famous Sharrowbay Hotel; or, if it's summer, you can catch an Ullswater Steamer to Howtown(Tel. 01768 482229 to check the times and dates). The back road can be busy which means waiting and reversing.

Martindale

There's a bay called Sandwick round the headland to the south from the pier that lets you off for Howtown. In 1850 a man called Jack Wilson lived at Sandwick Rigg and he saw a group of the fair folk. It was a moonlit night and he watched them playing around a ladder which went up into the clouds above. When they saw Wilson looking at them, they retreated up the ladder into fairy land. Though he ran, he couldn't catch them and they hastily pulled the ladder after them. That was traditionally the last time the fairies were seen in Cumbria.

If you've got off the boat at Howtown Pier or if you've driven, you need to take the road up the hill over into Martindale. You pass by the new church on your left, but keep on going. Ahead, down the long, narrow valley of Martindale lie the steep, and usually cloud wreathed, slopes of The Nab. Before you cross the beck you'll see the low, slate built church. Stop near here.

The church is very atmospheric. It's very simple, dedicated to St Martin, it was built in 1633 and the dark wooden altar table inside is also 17th century. There's no electricity and no adornment of any kind. On the pulpit and the pews are the remains of guttered out candles, which must be the only light at services held in winter.

From outside the church, if you look down across the flat ground of the valley bottom you'll see a small raise and a ruined farm building. This is Henhow and in 1857, Jeremiah Sullivan published the story of the Henhow Boggle. Sullivan dates the story to about 1834. He says that the man who lived at Henhow had temporary work at another farm some distance away, so he had to set off walking just after midnight. He hadn't got very far when he noticed the shape of a woman carrying a child keeping pace with him on the other side of the stone wall. His dog was very uneasy and he recalled his wife telling him about the strange noises she'd recently heard in their house.

Anyone living in Martindale knows everyone else living in Martindale; yet he didn't know her. As he got to the bridge, he asked her who she was and what was her business. She said she was dead, but had once lived at Henhow and had been seduced. She fell pregnant and the seducer agreed to do something about it. He met her in a nearby market town, either Penrith of Keswick, and gave her a potion to kill the child she was carrying.

Unfortunately, or perhaps deliberately, the medicine killed both her and her child and her spirit returned home to Henhow to haunt the lane and house for a hundred years. She said she'd already served forty years of her sentence, so it must have happened about 1796. She also said her seducer was a clergyman. After telling him her story she let him go on his way.

When he got home from work that night he told his wife and when word got out, some of his older neighbours recalled the incident exactly as the spirit had told it.

I was in Henhow in June 1998, a hundred and two years

after the girl's sentence was up and I was thinking about this story. There was no one else about and I walked alone round St Martin's church. Behind the church is an old yew tree and its branches have grown so that there's almost a green chamber close by the bole of the tree. There, sheltered by the boughs, is the green stained sepulchre of a clergyman who died about 1864. Despite the long time since his death, there was a wreath of newly dead flowers on it. I got the most unpleasant feeling, the strongest reaction from any place I'd been while researching this book. I thought: who would come and put flowers on the grave of a man who died one hundred and twenty four years ago?

At first I thought this might be the clergyman who seduced the young woman, but the years don't match up and, by the inscription, he was a paragon of virtue. The sensation probably arose from a combination of imagination, light conditions, remoteness and the image of the newly dead flowers on an old grave. Probably.

Leave Martindale and go all the way back to Pooley Bridge, drive back down to the lake on the other side, down the A592 in the direction of Glenridding and Patterdale. You pass by the National Trust site at Aira Force. There are legends associated with this place, and the tea room's supposed to have a ghost. Aira Force is popular with tourists, but worth a look if you've got time. Near the waterfall is a dead tree with branches twisted like the face of a Green Man.

Continue on through Glenridding and Patterdale and start to climb up the twisty road to Kirkstone Pass. You should be careful in winter if there's ice about and it's better not to attempt the drive in snowy conditions.

The Kirkstone Pass Inn

Crowded With Spirits

Tel. 01539 433624

Tariff (1999): £45 per room

This is the highest pub in Cumbria - 1500 feet above sea level. It stands right at the top of the pass, just before the road forks off for Windermere or Ambleside. It was built in the 1840s and before that time this road was very hard for the weary traveller and many died in the attempt. This area can enjoy brilliant sunshine but it has its fair share of snow and very often mists hang about the valley below the pub.

One story of the pass concerns Ruth Ray who came up from Patterdale and was on her way home after seeing her sick father. The snow began to fall and when she didn't return, her husband went out looking for her. He would have died, but he came across a sheepdog which led him to its master who had a rough dwelling nearby. In the morning the man and the shepherd set off to look for Ruth Ray. When they found her she was dead, but she'd wrapped the child in her shawl and by some miracle it still lived.

When I spoke to Pattie Yates, the owner of the inn, she told me that the ghost of Ruth Ray had been seen around the building, though not by her or her family.

A sign outside claims the Kirkstone Inn was originally built in 1496, but though that may be true it was a ruin for a long time until the middle of the last century. Now it's a warm and welcoming sight for sore eyes amongst for those with sore feet.

Pattie Yates said she'd never intended to run a pub, but had fallen in love with the building when she first saw it in 1988. Shortly after she moved in she was sitting in the snug when a man came and sat down near her. She realised that he was blind, and his wife was at the bar. He started talking to her straight away, seeming to know she was the new owner. He said the place was full of spirits, but that she shouldn't worry because none of them wished her any harm. When his wife returned, she told Pattie that he was a medium.

Since that time she's been at the Kirkstone Inn through storm and blizzard, with and without electric light, and has never once felt frightened. However, one or two guests take one step into the place and turn straight round again. Many people have reported feeling the presence of ghosts in the Kirkstone Pass Inn. On one occasion a group of friends booked all three rooms for three nights. In the middle of the first night one woman took fright and went out to sleep in the car. She wouldn't go back inside and the whole party left the next day, despite losing their deposit.

The inn certainly feels old and cosy. It's a long, low building with old black beams and a stone floor.

One of the tenant managers, Tracey Collings, reported a glass that flew across the room on its own and landed without smashing.

Another ghostly incident that made the local papers dates from July 1993. A family called Cave came for lunch one Spring day - father, mother and daughter. Though they lived away, Angela Cave was originally from Windermere and liked to come back to her family's home area. Apparently, when Brian Cave was at the bar, a man in an old fashioned black tricorn hat had come into the bar. His clothes looked as if they were from the 1700s, but Brian didn't like to say anything, not even to his wife.

Later on he took a photograph of his wife and daughter standing outside the door of the Kirkstone. He stood on the other side of the road to get the picture. The weather was fine and there was no one else about. However, when the photograph was developed, there was a man in a tricorn hat in it, standing behind his wife. Both he and she swear that there was no such man there with them when the photograph was taken. Another twist is that during the visit Angela had felt a pressure on her shoulder as if someone was gripping her. When she looked at the end of the day, she clearly saw red fingermarks against her skin.

This story in the paper prompted the recollection of a local man who came specially up to the Kirkstone to tell his tale. He was in his 60s in 1993 and he said when he was about sixteen he'd come up from Kendal with a local building firm to help put the new grate in. The pub was closed and his boss left him to get on with it while he went outside. The young lad worked away and then he thought he heard someone come in. Thinking it was his boss returning he didn't turn round. Then he began to feel frightened and when he looked up he was terrified to see a grey woman standing above him. She had no face and she was reaching out to touch him. He says that he doesn't remember how he got out past her, but he found himself outside on the road and couldn't be persuaded to go in again.

Another of the ghosts dates from the 1970s. There was a young man who worked there as a barman called Neville. Neville's great hobby was fell running so the Kirkstone was a great place for him to work. However, after he'd been there a while, he went out on one of his regular runs and didn't come back. The police and the mountain rescue searched for him for a long time but eventually gave up. He was found some months later, dead on the fell. He had a stone in his throat and it's thought he may have choked. It's fairly common practise for fell runners to have stones in their mouths to keep them from getting too dry.

However, before Neville's body was found, his ghost had already been seen by the staff. Neville doesn't mean anyone any harm, but he's known to leave doors open and move things around. He's particularly associated with Room 2. One woman who stayed in Room 2 came down one morning to report an 'ice cold thing' that had dragged its way over her feet.

This thing might not be Neville because, by all accounts, he was a very nice man and his wife and daughter visited Kirkstone in September 1998 and enjoyed being

there very much.

The final mysterious thing in the inn concerns a picture hanging there. It's a copy of an original in Troutbeck church. It's a picture of Rev. Sewell who built the inn in 1847. The strange thing is that in this copy there's the figure of a man standing behind Rev. Sewell; in the original, this other wasn't very clear and nobody had noticed it.

Outside the Inn, on the pass, there are very few trees. One of these is an old broken tree called the Hangman's Tree. The ghost of a woman's seen near this tree and the story is that she was hung there after being found guilty of murdering a child.

Because of its special position at the top of the pass and the real sense of it being a haven from the elements amongst the mountains, the Kirkstone is definitely worth a visit.

Troutbeck

Continue on the A592 towards Windermere. Look out for a sign to your right for The Mortal Man Inn. Take this road through the village of Troutbeck

I contacted The Mortal Man regarding ghosts, but if they had one they didn't want to tell me about it. The odd name was given about 1800 when a new sign was painted with a teetotaller and a supper talking to each other with balloons out of their mouths which read:

Thou mortal man, who liv'st by bread,
What is it makes thy nose so red?
Thou silly fool, that looks so pale,
'Tis drinking Sally Birkett's ale.

Troutbeck is a pretty village now though in the 1860s it was notable for its dirtiness and poverty.

Carrying on this road through the village will bring you to a T junction with the A591, the main Keswick to Windermere road. Turn left towards Windermere. Go through the hamlet of Troutbeck Bridge, past the Sun Inn. As you're coming into Windermere, look out for a turning on your right marked Old Hall Road, just before a bed and breakfast called Corner Cottage. This road's a dead end. You can go a little way down through the trees until you come to a right turn. Take this turn which goes with fields on your right but eventually comes to an stop in front of the gates of a farm. There's a path to your right. The ramshackle building to your left is in fact Calgarth Hall.

It has the appearance of a house that's been added to bit by bit over the centuries. All the windows are different shapes and sizes and it's been covered by a white rendering which is now coming off in places. It's private property but Pevsner got inside and describes it as a rambling farmhouse with a Jacobean interior.

In the 1600s it was the home of Robert Philipson, also known as Robert the Devil, who fought for the King during the English Civil War and was besieged on Belle Isle on Windermere. Calgarth Hall is more famous, however, because of the two skulls that were kept there.

A report of the skulls from 1788 by a man called James Clarke says that they belonged to two people that Robert had killed. Other versions of the story say that they were the skulls of Kraster and Dorothy Cook who owned land adjoining Calgarth. A previous owner of Calgarth called Myles Philipson coveted their land. He invited them over one Christmas and accused them of stealing a silver cup which he planted in their bags. They were tried and found guilty but at the point of her execution at Appleby, Dorothy cursed him seven times and promised that they'd haunt Calgarth day and night.

Their skulls came into the house and could never be banished. Every evening they were in the house, horrible unearthly groans, screams and moans would be heard, scaring the living daylights out of anyone nearby. They were burnt, smashed, doused with quicklime and carried away, but they always returned whole to Calgarth.

The luck of the Philipsons did wither away and they died out. In 1819 a tourist guide reported that there was only one skull left. The estate was bought by the Bishop of Llandaff and he exorcised the skulls and had them bricked up on the walls. After that they troubled the place no more.

We have seen another guardian skull at Threlkeld and another at Brougham Hall. We have seen ancient Celtic heads that were built into the walls of a farm near Wigton. It's well known the ancient inhabitants of Cumbria and other parts of Britain and western Europe had a cult of the head. Until modern times, having a carved head, or even a skull, in the house was thought to protect it. These objects were spirits in their own right and if not treated with the proper respect, they could cause trouble.

In *Twilight of the Celtic Gods*, David Clarke has a whole chapter on supernatural skulls from Lancashire and the South West of England. He says there that: 'Guardian skulls are a little known aspect of British folk lore... In the Peak District, Northwest England and the West Country, ancient and mysterious human skulls have been associated with the "luck of the house" for centuries, a belief which dates back to Celtic times.'

Clarke refers to a particular skull from Bettiscome in Dorset which was said to date from the 1700s, but which, upon examination was found to be between 3,000 and 4,000 years old. Though folk belief may give them a more modern date and a convincing story, the truth might well be that the Calgarth skulls were cult objects dating from any time from the 1600s back to the Stone Age.

Nab Ferry

Go back to the main road. Turn right for Windermere and then at the roundabout take the right for Bowness on Windermere. Follow the signs for the ferry. This is a very pleasant car ferry that takes you across the lake. On the Bowness side is a building that was once the Ferry Inn. In the old days the ferry was a rowing boat and strange stories were told about winter nights on this part of Windermere.

There are local stories that are similar to tales of the Wild Hunt or the Gabriel Hounds, unearthly dogs that hunt at the command of the Lord of the Beasts, whatever name he's known by - Herne, Cernunnos or Arawn. And when the wind howls down the lake it's easy to imagine the baying of the hounds and the horn of the huntsman.

One story refers to the Crier of Claife. Claife is the wooded area with an old quarry on the far side of the Lake. Legend has it that on odd nights a voice called out *'Boat! Boat!'* from the Claife side. Most of the boatmen were wise enough to ignore it, but on one wild and stormy night one of them, brave or foolhardy, chose to row over to answer the voice. After about half an hour, he returned with an empty boat but he was so terrified that he couldn't talk. His friends did their best for him, but by the next morning he was dead.

All sorts of stories circulated about Claife which was said to be the haunt of demons and witches. Then, a monk persuaded someone to row him across the lake with bell and bible in his hands. When he landed he went into the woods of Claife and found the demon in the old quarry. By the power of his faith, he caused it to be bound 'until men should walk dryshod across the lake.'

That doesn't seem to be the end of it however, because in fairly recent times there's the story of a fox hunt coming to Claife, and the hounds suddenly came to a dead stop and couldn't be persuaded to go any further. There was also a schoolmaster from Colthouse who laughed at the stories of the demon at Claife and went out one night to show what nonsense it all was. He was never seen again.

One explanation of who the Crier of Claife was, is that he was a monk from Furness Abbey, who in the Middle Ages, became involved with a local woman. He loved the woman deeply but because of his position could never marry her. In the end she married someone else and he went up to the wilderness of Claife to die of grief.

You can walk onto the heights of Claife, through the trees, but be warned - there are stories of walkers being followed in mist or at dusk by a hooded figure.

There's also another story about Windermere. When grievous harm's about to come to the neighbourhood, a spectral white horse can be seen walking on the water from shore to shore.

Once you're over the lake, take the road for Far Sawrey. On the Sawrey road, near the ferry, you may see the gibbeted ghost of Thomas Lancaster, the poisoner from Threlkeld.

Go through Far Sawrey and onto Hawkshead, then follow the road to Ambleside.

Ambleside

The only ghost story I have found about Ambleside is from Charlotte Mason's College on the right hand side of the road as you head for Keswick. Before it was a College, it was a hotel and in the early years of this century there was a fire in the hotel. Many of the staff were burned to death and the building's still supposed to smell of their charred flesh on occasions.

Go through Ambleside on the A591 in the direction of Keswick. You'll soon pass by Rydal Water, where Wordsworth stole a boat one summer night, and then you'll see signs off to the left for Grasmere. Grasmere is a pretty, and much visited village, which has a ghost story from one of the local pubs. Gerald Findler records this from the middle 1960s. He says that some locals were in a pub in the village talking about ghosts. A stranger joined in the conversation. The locals said 'We've been talking about ghosts, but we don't believe in them.' At which point the stranger vanished.

Go back onto the A591 and head up towards Keswick. Soon you'll come to a short stretch of dual carriageway.

The tall mountains gather around on both sides and in the central reservation area between the carriageways is a large heap of stones - a cairn. This was the spot where the last king of Cumbria died in battle against the English. He was called Dunmail, which is probably a corruption of Dumnual, meaning 'world ruler'.

Dunmail's father was Owain who haunts Dacre castle. Owain signed a peace treaty with the King of England in 927, but by 945 there was a new king of Anglo-Saxon England - Edmund. Edmund decided to teach the Cumbrians a lesson and he attacked from the south. Dunmail resisted him and the legend has it that as he lay dying he took of his crown and cried 'My crown - bear it away. Never let the Saxon flaunt it.' His sons took the crown and other symbols of the Cumbrian royal house and fled up the mountains to the right of the cairn until they got to Grisedale Tarn. There they threw the crown into the dark waters.

They were later captured by the English and blinded and castrated so there would be no more kings of Cumbria.

Dunmail's supposed to be buried beneath the cairn - sleeping until he's called to deliver Cumbria from her enemies. Each year, the ghosts of his sons go to Grisedale Tarn and bring him the crown and ask if he will awake. Each year he answers, 'No, not yet. Wait a while.'

There was a report to a newspaper in 1949 that two women had climbed up to Grisedale Tarn the same way as Dunmail's sons - up between Seat Sandal and the Dollywaggon. They heard the voices of men in front of them, but could see no one. At the top they searched for the source of the voices but found nobody there.

Continue on the road, over Dunmail Raise and down towards Keswick. Watch out for the small, abrupt turn on your left that takes you on the west side of Thirlmere.

Take this turn and continue up the west bank of the lake between the forest and the lake edge. About three quarters of the way up you'll come to a place called

Armboth. North West Water have created a car park down a track to the right. This marks the edge of the lands that belonged to the estate of Armboth. There once was a house here which is now drowned under the waters of Thirlmere. If you look across the water you'll see Dale Head Hall.

Armboth was supposed to be the most haunted house in Cumbria. In 1854 Harriet Martineau wrote a book called *The Complete Guide to the English Lakes*. She said Armboth was a haunted house where lights were seen at night and where bells would mysteriously ring. A large ghostly dog was seen swimming across the lake but inside the house the plates and dishes clattered as a wedding feast was set out by ghostly hands. The bride arose from the waters where she was drowned and came to her wedding feast.

But the apparitions only occurred on Halloween. In 1905 an account of Halloween at Armboth said that all the phantoms of Cumbria gather there - including the skulls of Calgarth. If you continue up the road by the lake from Armboth and bear right over the Victorian dam, you'll eventually find yourself at a junction with the A591. Turn right and you'll soon see the turning for Dale Head Hall to the right.

The Western Lakes

Hotel: Gosforth Hall

The Priest's Hole

Tel. 01946 725322

Tariff (1999): £35

Getting There:

From Junction 40 of the M6, take the A66 west towards Workington. Some six miles short of Workington turn left onto the A595 towards Whitehaven. Continue on through Whitehaven, past Egremont. Take the left turn off the main road into the village of Gosforth. Go through Gosforth and take the left for Wasdale. Gosforth Hall hotel is on your left shortly after the turn.

Gosforth Hall was built in 1658 by a local gentleman called Robert Copley. Copley is recorded as having lived in Gosforth in 1653, but in another house. He was obviously a bit of a cheapskate, because he wouldn't pay the Royal Herald for his own coat of arms, so he made one up which can be seen in the modern bar.

The Hall has an atmosphere from the minute you enter the Renaissance gate posts; the floors are uneven, the doorways low and there's a fantastic stone spiral stair case. One strange thing you'll encounter climbing the stairs is a font. It's a modern font and what it's doing there, I was unable to find out. In the wall of the staircase is a stoup for holy water.

There's also a priest's hole which leads down from Room 11 to the fireplace in the bar. In 17th Century England, it was difficult to be a Catholic. There was great suspicion of 'popery'. It might well be then that Robert Copley and his wife Isabella were Catholics and they had

WORKINGTON
COCKERMOUTH
A66
HIGH HARRINGTON
A595
A5086
MORESBY
ARLECDON
ROWRAH
WHITEHAVEN
CLEATOR MOOR
EGREMONT
ST BEES
WAST WATER
GOSFORTH
STANTON BRIDGE
HOLMROOK
ESKDALE GREEN
MUNCASTER CASTLE
A595

to be careful about revealing that fact.

Room 11 has a large old four poster bed and it's here that surprised guests have woken in the night to see a ghostly figure sitting near the priest's hole. He's very indistinct but some guests have reported that he was wearing a religous habit like monk or a friar.

There's another tradition that Copley built the upper stories of Gosforth Hall out of the timbers of ships wrecked on the nearby Irish Sea. Legend has it that those timbers groan with the spirits of the poor souls who drowned when the ships went down, lasting as long as they could clinging to the flotsam, before finally breathing their last.

In the early 1990s there were lots of contractors in this part of Cumbria building the Thorp Reprocessing plant. Staff working at the Hall at that time have told me that many who stayed in Room 11 reported odd things happening to them.

There have been other ghostly happenings at the Hall. Locals talk about a chair that's been seen gently rocking by the large Jacobean fireplace in the lounge area and the sound of footsteps in unoccupied rooms. There's also a face that appears at the upstairs windows, somehow suspended in mid air as it peers in at guests.

One lady who worked in the kitchen at Gosforth Hall told me that, on occasions, pewter tankards would unhook themselves in full view of everyone and fly across the bar.

The current manager, Diane Morgan, moved into the hotel in early 1998. She told me that there's an old gentleman who wafts through the small bar area. She hasn't seen him herself, but her staff have. Her only ghostly experience so far was when she and one of the staff were cleaning the bar one morning in early summer. Suddenly there was a gust of very cold wind. The maid looked up at Diane in surprise. The doors and windows were closed and it was otherwise a mild day.

For some reason there's no room 8 in the hotel. The numbering jumps from 7 to 9. One story has it that the ghostly monk's still around because he's looking for room 8.

Above Gosforth Hall is a field called Chapel Meadow. In this meadow, are the ruins of an ancient chapel. There's a basin inside the chapel from which a holy spring flows. When the water was tested, it was found to have certain beneficial minerals, and traditionally on religious feast days, particularly those that commemorated old pagan festivals, the locals would gather at the spring and pour in red wine. They'd then drink this mixture of spring water and wine and it was supposed to bring health and good luck.

In the churchyard of St Mary's Church near Gosforth Hall hotel is the famous Gosforth Cross. The Church has parts dating from the 14th Century, but the Cross is dated to the late 900s. It's one of the finest examples of the work of the Vikings who settled in these parts after spending years in Ireland. It has the typical wheeled cross head and scroll work that you see in Irish gospels from this period, but the carvings round the bottom seem to be pagan Norse in origin.

According to one theory the tree on the cross represents Yggdrasil - the World Tree that supports the universe. On the west side, there's a bound figure which may be Christ or it may be the god Loki. According to the pagan interpretation, this is Loki, bound as a punishment and above him is the gape of a venomous snake. Loki's wife Sigyn stands below catching the poison that falls from the snake in a bowl.

On the same western face as Loki, there's the god Odin riding forth to the well of wisdom, fighting off the demon wolf serpents Skoll and Hati.

On the South side we see Odin again riding through the hall of the serpents where the wolf and the serpent attack a hart, a symbol of good.

On the east side is Odin hanging on the tree, self sacrificed.

On the north side is much interlacing and the figure of Odin battling the giant Surtur in the battle of Ragnarok - the end of the world.

There's also a triskele, an Irish symbol of Eternity.

One other feature of the Church at Gosforth is the doors in the north wall. These are called Devil Doors and are found in many Cumbrian churches. Taditionally when a baby was baptised, they'd be opened to allow the evil spirits to depart to their home in the cold, barren north.

Wasdale

If you head west from Gosforth you enter the valley of Wasdale. It's a long and winding road, but it leads to the deepest lake in England, and certainly the most dramatic. This is the undiscovered Lake District and very quiet. The weather's often inclement and the steep scree covered slopes on the southern shore of the lake quite awe inspiring.

Wastwater is the deepest lake because the slope continues at that same angle from the mountainside down into the cold, deoxygenated depths. In fact, in the 1960s an airline pilot killed his wife and threw her into the deep water. She wasn't found for twenty years; but when she was pulled out, her body was perfectly preserved.

At the end of the Wasdale Valley is Wasdale Head, a small collection of farms and a pub. The pub's white-washed and can be seen from far away. There's a small church named after St Olaf in commemoration of the area's Norse links. However, this is very recent and for all the previous centuries the people of Wasdale had to carry their dead over the mountains into the next valley on the appropriately named Corpse Road.

The Corpse Road climbs over Burn Moor into Eskdale. These corpse roads are found in many of the remote valleys. They were traditional routes that weren't deviated from for fear of bad luck.

One particular time, a young man died and his body was

strapped to a horse to be carried over into Eskdale. The weather was bad and the clouds were down. These mountains are very dangerous in bad weather. Near the top, something spooked the horse carrying the body and it bolted. The funeral group tried to catch it but the horse disappeared into the swirling mist and was lost.

The young man's mother took it badly and went in a low way; she pined and wouldn't eat, and eventually died. In due course, her body was carried on horseback over the corpse road. The winter had deepened and there was much snow on the ground. Halfway over Burn Moor, a blizzard came suddenly on them. The funeral party could go on no further and had to retreat down into the valley. In the poor visibility the horse with the woman's corpse was lost. The woman was never found, though a search party eventually came across the dead bodies of her son and his horse caught in a crevice.

It's said travellers on that lonely way come across a mad horse galloping towards them with the body of an old woman strapped to its back, banging wildly up and down, as it hurtles over the rocks and grass.

The Screes Hotel

Nether Wasdale

Tel. 01946 726262

Tariff (1999): £20 - £28 B&B

Nether Wasdale is a remote hamlet in the middle of some amazing scenery. The centre of the village consists of three small walkers' hotels and a couple of farmhouses.

The morning I arrived (Saturday, 12 September 1998) an Australian couple had just checked out due to the ghostly activities of the night before. No one had told them that the room they were staying in, Room 4, was haunted; they'd had to find out for themselves.

About one o'clock in the morning, their television fizzled out and a strange atmosphere filled the room. The man reported that he'd had gone out of the room earlier that evening and something had held the door closed against him coming back. Suddenly it released the door and, ill at ease, he went to bed.

Late at night he heard footsteps on the landing and a repeated tapping at his door. That was enough for him and his girlfriend; though they'd booked for two nights, they left after only one.

Room 4 has a history of minor hauntings, as does Room 3 next door to it, but from the flood of stories that came from the staff in the inn, the ghost, or ghosts are obviously very active.

They showed me the men's toilets that adjoin the bar area. The door handle had a crack in it where they'd broken it open. It's a fairly unremarkable modern toilet cubicle with no room above or below the door to squeeze out. One particular evening the cubicle door was locked from the inside and remained locked for some time. Becoming concerned, the barman went outside and saw that the window was still shut. After a while they broke the door down, fearing that someone might have been taken ill. There was no one there.

The ghost's often felt in the bar area by the staff and also by the old back door which leads into the kitchen. One of the young barmaids told me that she'd once been in the bar and had heard all the cutlery in the drawers in the kitchen moving around. There was no one in the kitchen at the time, and even if there had been, it's difficult to see how the knives and forks in different drawers could be moved at once.

As recently as 1997, beer glasses were known to extract themselves from the drawer under the bar and turn in perfect circles in mid air before coming gently to rest on the ground.

The previous owner, Moira, was once making the bed in her private room when she saw a pair of shiny black shoes with silver buckles on the floor on the other side of the bed. They looked very old fashioned and she was curious because they weren't her husband's. She walked round to pick them up, but when she got the other side of the bed they'd gone.

This is significant because the presence in the bar has shown himself on occasions. He only lets you see him if he likes you, and he's described as having dark hair, an old fashioned white shirt with a large collar and black shiny-buckled shoes.

In the 1920s and 1930s the Screes was a Temperance Hotel. According to the present staff, the hauntings only started when the licence to serve alcohol was granted. Maybe the ghost doesn't like people drinking.

The current manager's partner, Sylvia Mercer, was once staying in a room on the ground floor in the modern part of the house when she was awoken in the early hours by an almighty crash. The double doors, which were bolted, had both been flung wide open and knocked over the ladder that was standing against them. She admits to have been drinking that night, so perhaps that was the cause of the ghost's disapproval.

Egremont

Return to Gosforth and turn right onto the A595 in the direction of Whitehaven. Continue on along the A595 until you come to the start of the Egremont by-pass. Turn left at the first roundabout and a small road takes you into the town. On your left you'll see the wooded hill upon which the castle ruins stand. Egremont's one of the old boroughs of Cumbria and the hill is a Norman motte.

There are some find old buildings in Egremont and Nikolaus Pevsner in his Cumberland & Westmorland volume of the buildings of England called the high street '...quite a handsome sight for an industrial Cumberland town.'

West Cumbria has suffered a lot of deprivation since the early years of this century, but underneath the dirt, there's a lot of interest here. In 1802, Coleridge visited

Egremont and wrote a beautiful description of it. He called the view of the town from the Castle 'a dream'.

The castle was built by Norman barons, but you'll also see a pub called *The Horn of Egremont*. The heir to the barony of Egremont was captured and held to ransom by his enemies. However, his brother back home refused to pay the ransom and took his brother's place as baron. The poor captive was hung by his hair from a beam.

However, the captor's daughter fell in love with the prisoner and cut him down with a knife. As she did so, she cut off the skin of his scalp. The lovers ran away, and after a while came to Egremont where the brother was feasting in the Great Hall. Suddenly, by itself, the Horn of Egremont rang out clear and true. The Horn could only be blown by the true heir to the barony and the usurper, realising the game was up, sprang up and welcomed his brother - the true baron - home.

If you're in Egremont on Christmas Eve, you may see the ghostly pony rider. This is also an old story from the Middle Ages. One Christmas Eve a hill farmer came in from the surrounding fells and took too much ale. Some accident must have befallen him on his way home, because he was never seen again. The ghost of rider and pony haunt the streets every Christmas.

Gerald Findler in his *Ghosts of the Lake Counties* reports the story of Egremont's haunted tannery. It's not a tannery any more but still exists. The story is that a local police sergeant was in a pub one night when his son and three other lads came in looking pretty shaky. They said they'd been playing about in the Tannery and had seen a ghost. Gathering a group together, the police sergeant went to look and, near the Tannery, saw a white mist just above ground level. As he watched, it rose up and took the form of a body lacking head and feet. It started to float down the road towards the Tannery door and when it got there another ghostly figure appeared. Some of the people became very frightened and threw stones at the shapes but they went straight through. Then both ghosts suddenly went through the Tannery door. The investigators lost their nerve and didn't try to get into the Tannery. Though people scoffed, nine people testified to what they'd seen.

St Mary's Church was largely rebuilt in the 1880s. However in the churchyard near the west door are fragments of old sculpture. One of them looks very much like what, in Ireland, they call a Sheela na Gig. It's difficult to make out, but it seems to be a barbaric carving of a female figure with both hands holding her vulva apart. In ancient Ireland Sheela na Gigs are fertility symbols. It could have come from Ireland or have been carved by one of the Irish settlers who came to this part of Cumbria in the Dark Ages.

Rejoin the by-pass and go in the direction of Whitehaven until you come to the roundabout that signposts Cockermouth along the A5086. This takes you through the old iron mining villages of Cleator and Cleator Moor. As you go through Cleator you'll see the Roman Catholic church of Our Lady of the Sacred Heart with its very ornate stonework and grotto. It actually looks like something you would find in Ireland and in fact this area has a very large Catholic community of Irish descent. They came searching for work in the hard times in the last century and are still looking.

Arlecdon

Stay on the road and go through Frizington then continue on towards Arlecdon. On a clear day there are some wonderful views of the fells to the right hand side of the road and to the left some distance below you is the sea and, if the weather's clear, the Isle of Man.

Arlecdon is just off the main road adjoining Rowrah. It a poor mining village, but there's a good story about its church. Apparently in the early years of the last century - before 1829 at least - the people of Arlecdon wanted to build a church. The place they chose was called Jackson's Meadow. Every day they built the foundations and walls and every evening they went home. Always when they returned the next day, they found their work had been thrown down and dug up. They tried day after day, and when they posted people to watch, they heard a great roaring and rushing and ran away in terror. It became clear that some evil spirit was trying to destroy their work. In the end they took the hint and moved off to build the church of St Michael (note the dedication to the fighting archangel) in its current position.

Cockermouth

Continue on the road in the direction of Cockermouth and once you're out of Rowrah you'll feel yourself in the countryside again. This road skirts the National Park to the right. You go past Mockerkin Tarn, under which is the drowned village of Thorp Morken. It was drowned because of the evil ways of King Morken who persecuted the good Saint Mungo.

Continue on - the pretty villages (such as Ullock, Dean and Greysouthen) and countryside (Loweswater and the Vale of Lorton) near here are very peaceful and very beautiful if you've time for a diversion.

Cockermouth is the old capital of Allerdale (the barony based on the valley of the river Ellen). It has a broad main street and is a nice place to wander round - especially down by the river or near the church and old Free Grammar school. It was the birthplace of William and Dorothy Wordsworth and Fletcher Christian of the *Mutiny on the Bounty* fame came from nearby Eaglesfield.

Both Wordsworth and Christian were at the Free Grammar School at the same time, though Wordsworth was a little younger. Kirkgate is the street down from the church. It's very pretty and there's a pub that brews its own beer and an award winning vegetarian restaurant. The only ghosts that I've found out about near here aren't in

Cockermouth but around the old Roman site at Papcastle, where a friend of a girl I know swears he saw a ghostly Roman legionary.

Workington

Take the A66 and head west to Workington. Workington is said to be ugly, but the first description of it in 1540 describes it as a little pretty fisher town. Despite the heavy industry that's gone on there in the meantime, if you travel from Cockermouth on the A66 you'll not see much to offend the eye.

Come in through Stainburn, past Stainburn School to your left. Go up the hill and when you see the park on your right, look for a left turn. This will take you into an attractive cobbled area called Portland Square. This, and the streets around it, were once the polite area of town, though now their splendours are a little faded. Despite that, this slightly down at heel appearance gives them a certain charm. There's a hotel in the square called *The Green Dragon*. The Green Dragon used to be the posting house and the town hearse was kept in the stables there. There's a story that sometimes a hearse pulled by jet black horses is seen in the square. If you're there on a misty night and see such a thing, beware! It's a bad omen, but only for the residents of the Square, because when the hearse is seen, one of them is going to die.

There's also a good restaurant just down from Portland Square called the Townhouse.

Near Portland Square is Curwen Street. Once again, some nice houses in need of a bit of love. You can see that they're large town houses with big back gardens. My father was born in one of these and he told me that it was haunted. Once, after his father died, he was outside and looked up at the window where the old man habitually sat, and he saw the back of his head quite clearly, just as if he'd still been alive. There were other bumps in the night in the house, but nothing else was seen.

If you continue over the main road from Curwen Street, you come to the park. You'll see the shell of Workington Hall. This Hall has a bit of a history. It was the home of the de Curwens, who were descended from Earl Gospatric, pre Norman lord of this part of Cumbria and descended from the ancient Cumbrian Kings. Originally the Curwens had their castle at Burrow Walls, closer to the sea, but in 1362 they built a pele tower against the Scots on the hill where the ruin is today.

The Curwens prospered during Tudor times and the Hall became very grand. Its most famous visitor was Mary Queen of Scots. She escaped from her sister, Elizabeth in 1568 and fled from Scotland, crossing the Solway in a fishing boat. She was given safe haven by the Curwens. Many of the Cumbrian nobility were still Catholics in those days. After only one night, Elizabeth brought her influence to bear and Mary was led off to captivity again in Carlisle. However in her gratitude she gave Sir Henry Curwen an agate cup. This was the Luck of Workington and was kept by the Curwens until the line died out.

A descendent of Henry Curwen was also called Henry, but he was known as Galloping Harry. He was a Jacobite rebel in 1715. After his death, Galloping Harry Curwen's spirit lingered on. After the Curwens gave up the Catholic faith, Harry's portrait was kept facing the wall. This upset the spirit and he began to haunt the Hall. The haunting was the sound of a head bumping down the stairs. This was a particularly significant noise because when Harry was very ill, there was a French noblewoman staying at the hall. Seeing that he was close to death, she thought she would hasten him on his way by pulling him downstairs by the heels, his head bouncing on every step. She then ran off with all the jewellery she could get her hands on. Later on, the lady's maid came back to Workington and told that the thieving noblewoman had been shipwrecked off the Scilly Isles on her way back to France. The woman and the jewellery had gone down but the maid had survived.

Suitably chastised, she went into a nunnery and came back to Workington fifteen years later to confess her part in the crime.

In the 1950s, after the Curwens and their guests had been shooting in the High Woods, a group of them, including Reverend Patricius Lamplugh Curwen, sat in the library taking a drink. The spaniels lay warming themselves in front of the fire and then, during a lull in the conversation, the dogs suddenly started growling. They got up and stared at a door in the corner of the room. The door was an odd one because it was cut into one of the large pictures on the wall and, as the assembled group watched, it opened slowly on its own.

Though the humans could see nothing, the dogs followed with their eyes as something invisible moved from the door and sat down in a chair. After a short while the dogs watched the thing get out of the chair and go back to the door. The door opened wide again and then closed - by itself.

There are also stories of ghostly children who have been seen playing in the castle courtyard.

Turn the car round and head out of Workington. Take a right turn by the Helena Thompson Museum on Park End Road and follow the signs for Whitehaven. This road takes you out of Workington, up past the golf course. Turn right for High Harrington.

High Harrington and Lowca

This is Scaw Road. Scaw is an old Norse for 'wood' and the wood's still there. There's an unpleasant feel to that wood, and if you walk round it you'll get the strong impression that someone's watching you. Just before the road goes down into a depression with trees on both sides, if you can find it, there's a gravestone amongst the grass on the bank on the right hand side. This dates from the 1700s and records the burial place of a farm labourer's thumb. He cut it off with a scythe. The thumb is buried there but the rest of him went on to be buried somewhere else. This was actually quite a common thing to do in earlier times all over Britain. If part of you died, it had to be given a Christian burial.

If you continue on along Scaw Road you'll come to a mini roundabout at the Galloping Horse pub. Turn left here. After about a kilometre, take the small road signposted Parton. Follow that through the mining village of Lowca. You're close to the sea again.

There was once a huge slag bank at Lowca though it's now reclaimed and covered with grass. Towards the end of my grandfather's working life as a miner, he worked at Lowca pit. He told me a ghost story from deep underground.

Another miner whose name I don't know, but we can call John, told my grandfather that he had a friend who he'd worked with in the 1930s. As the shift finished, he met this friend in the cage that took them to the surface. John said his friend had a strange look on his face. John made some joke about it. The friend nodded and smiled but wouldn't say what the matter was, though he was obviously pleased with himself. During the course of the next day he told John that he'd seen a woman down the mine, that there was something about this woman that was very attractive and that he wanted to go down and see her again.

John told him not to be daft; how could there be a beautiful woman down a pit? But the friend was adamant; he wanted to see this woman again. And furthermore, he wanted to go down at night when there was nobody else around. He asked John to go with him. Of course, at first John refused, but as the days went by and the friend played on his loyalty and called him a coward, he gave in.

So, when there was no one else working, in breach of all the safety rules, they got themselves down in the cage to the bottom of the shaft. Although the way was very familiar and night or day didn't make much difference down the pit, it felt odd. The mine was much quieter than when a shift was working. John said he began to feel strangely nervous but his friend was very keen to go on. John said there was a mad gleam in his eye, as he walked quickly onwards towards the gallery where he said he'd seen the woman.

Eventually they got there. There was nothing to be seen. John was all for going back, but his friend wanted to stay. Five minutes stretched to half an hour. John said again, 'Let's go back now. There's nothing here.' But then he saw his friend stand up, listening. He listened himself and he heard it. The rustling of silk - a sound very alien in such a dark place so far underground. John began to get very scared and he pulled at his friend to go. The man turned round, smiling, and said, 'I knew she'd come'. John grabbed at him to try and get him to leave but his friend knocked his arms away. John could hear the rustling of silk again, getting closer. He knew something wasn't right. He started back, walked away. He called for his friend to come, but he stayed put. Miners are big strong men, not given much to imagining, but John said he was scared out of his wits. He heard the sound again and he turned and ran.

The next day his friend was found dead, not far from where he'd left him: inexplicably dead, without a mark on his body. The authorities presumed that he must have been overcome by gas the previous day and somehow over-looked and left down there.

From Lowca you head down the hill. Standing out alone is Moresby Church. This is on the right. On the left hand side of the road is Moresby Hall.

Moresby

Moresby Church stands on the site of a Roman fort built in 128. From this fort was dug the bust of a Celtic horned god. The church is dedicated to the Irish saint, or goddess,

Bridget. There was a medieval church here but the only remains of it are a single arch standing in the churchyard.

One October night in 1997, a local woman was walking her golden retriever dog. She told me this story herself, but doesn't want to be named. She said she'd often walked the dog in the churchyard and this particular night, she sat down on the seaward side of the church to admire the stars which were particularly clear and bright. The dog sniffed around the gravestones as usual, but suddenly it ran towards her, as if for protection, and turned growling towards the arch. She started to get scared herself and as she looked in the direction the dog was gazing she saw a shape - a gaseous kind of shape, sulphurous yellow in colour, rising out of the ground. It was broadly the shape of a human being but there was something very awful about it.

Both she and the dog started to run. The dog was so scared that it emptied its bowels. They got out of the churchyard onto the road and ran up the hill towards Lowca. As they passed by the road that cuts down the hill to Parton they saw the yellow shape suddenly appear in the grass there. In absolute terror they ran up the hill. It seems that the shape couldn't follow them. Now, at about that point, the road crosses over a stream. You don't appreciate you're crossing water at first because the bridge doesn't look like a bridge at first sight. It may be that this creature couldn't cross running water.

Moresby Hall's on the other side of the road from the Church. The facade is from 1690 or so but behind this is a heart dating from medieval times - another pele tower. Moresby Hall has just changed hands and when I spoke to the new owner she told me some interesting things. When the Hall was being renovated for her to move in, a new stone floor was put down and the old one taken up. Underneath the contractors found the remains of eight people. The police soon passed the case onto the local archaeological unit who said they were of Roman date and probably came from a cemetery associated with the near-by Fort.

Nikolaus Pevsner mentions the huge chimney breast inside the Hall, but the new owner told me that when the hall was being renovated in early 1998, the chimney breast was opened up and inside was revealed the skeleton of a child.

In 1715 a family called Fletcher owned the Hall and they supported the Jacobite rebels. When the Old Pretender finally lost, the Hanoverian Authorities took Squire Fletcher to London and questioned him about his treason. However, Fletcher forgot to tell his servants at Moresby, that in the cellar underneath the Hall there was another Jacobite in hiding. This is the traditional story at least, but Moresby Hall doesn't have a cellar and the local version is that the poor man was locked in a chest and couldn't get out. In due course he starved to death and his ghost still haunts the hall. There's a rumour that there's a tunnel under the road from the Hall to the church so that the Fletchers wouldn't get wet when they went to church.

Go back on the main road to Whitehaven. Whitehaven is an interesting town with some good Georgian buildings and a fascinating seafaring tradition. There are strong links with George Washington and the first American Navy, but there are few ghosts there that I have uncovered, so we must go on through Whitehaven to St Bees.

St Bees

At the heart of St Bees is the Abbey of St Mary & St Bega. It was founded in around 650 by the Irish saint Bega. The story is that she fled from Ireland away from a forced marriage. Some stories say to a Viking, but this is too early for Vikings, so it must have been an Irish nobleman. She was found wandering by the Lord of this part of Cumbria, his name isn't known, but he could have been one of the proud descendants of Coel Hen, or Old King Cole as he's better known in nursery rhymes. The Coelings were a very prolific family and seem to have had branches all over the place.

The Lord, whoever he was, took pity on Bega and said she could have all land covered by snow by the next morning. The snow very rarely lies in St Bees - it's too close to the sea. However, because she was a pious woman, and through the grace of God, when the next day dawned the whole valley was under a blanket of the white stuff.

The Abbey was burned by the Danes, and then refounded by the Normans in the 1100s. It was finally dissolved in 1539 by Henry VIII, keen to get his hands on the church's wealth.

The Abbey continues as a church and in it you'll see the story of the famous St Bees man. In 1981, this medieval knight was uncovered on the site of a ruined chapel. He was so well preserved that archaeologists were able to tell what he'd had for breakfast on the day he died.

St Bees has an old public school which was founded by an Archbishop of Canterbury, during the reign of Queen Elizabeth I. William Grindall was born in 1517 at a house in Finkle Street in the village - there's a plaque on the building commemorating the fact. The school prospered when coal was discovered underneath it and the Lowthers had to pay mineral rights to them before they could extract it.

The village of St Bees lies to the south of the Abbey and the school and is full of little alleys and interesting buildings built of the local red sandstone. There's an old pub there called The Queen's Hotel. It has a ghost.

The Queens Hotel

Tel. 01946 822287

Tariff (1999): £30 B&B

The pub is actually three cottages joined together. It has an old fashioned reception desk to the left as you go in and the whole place has the intimate feel of someone's home. There's a restaurant with lots of dark wood and candles and the managers are extremely welcoming. I was unable to find out the exact date of the cottages that make up The Queen's Hotel, or when it actually became a hotel. The place is stone built and could in fact date from the days of Elizabeth I, whose head adorns the sign outside.

The ghost haunts Room 11 and is on the whole very well behaved. He annoys Joyce, the cleaner, by messing up beds she's just made. She says that she knows that he's been around because the beds look as if someone's been rolling around on them. The manageress, Kay Steele, tells me that on many occasions guests will report for breakfast and ask her if their room, Room 11, is haunted. On the whole they're interested and amused, but on one occasion a businessman was staying in the hotel midweek and came down rather ashen faced. He said he'd woken in the night to hear a voice asking him, 'What are you doing here?'

Apart from that the ghost, whose name's unknown, restricts himself to walking around at night letting people hear his footsteps and moving small things around.

Continue south through St Bees, on the main road to Gosforth. This time, don't turn into Gosforth but keep going straight on. You go through the pretty village of Holmrook and you'll see the Lutwidge Arms to your right. This hotel has no ghost, but it's on the site of Holmrook Hall; the family seat of the Lutwidges - cousins of Lewis Carroll (real name: Charles Lutwidge Dodgson) the author of the Alice in Wonderland books. He visited Holmrook often in the 1870s.

The countryside continues to get prettier, but keep on the main road until you come to the sign for Ravenglass.

Ravenglass

There's a dead end road into the delightful village of Ravenglass. The old hotel, the Pennington Arms, is currently closed, awaiting refurbishment, but is apparently full of ghosts.

Ravenglass is at the mouth of three rivers and at one

time must have almost been almost an island. It's the site of yet another Roman fort; an important sea port where ships loaded copper brought out from the central fells. The remains of a Roman bath house can still be seen along a road which isn't a right of way for vehicles.

Ravenglass is very sleepy now, but in the Middle Ages the remains of the Bath House were known as Lyons Garde and were said to be the home of the Arthurian Fairy - Morgana La Fée. One author suggests that after Arthur fought his last battle at Camlann (Birdoswald near Carlisle?), he was brought along the Roman road to the Solway Firth and taken by ship to Ravenglass - the Isle of Avalon. An early name for Ravenglass was Aveling Glas - 'Green Avalon'

Muncaster Castle

This historic castle and splendid gardens are open to the public. There's an admission charge.

Muncaster has the reputation of being the most haunted castle in England and has featured on a number of television programmes. One of the programmes that did an extensive piece on Muncaster was the ITV series '*Strange But True?*'.

Muncaster' s name suggests that the site has Roman origins, but despite strong rumours that underneath the pele tower there's a Roman fort, little evidence has been found. There are gorgeous views from the front of the castle over the valley of the River Esk and across to the fells beyond. There's also an international owl centre and places to eat. The Castle and the estate have been owned by the Pennington family for many centuries and the family still lives there.

There are certainly lots of ghosts at Muncaster. In the casebook that accompanied the *Strange But True?* TV series, the present owner Patrick Gordon-Duff-Pennington reported that strange things were still happening. He said, 'I went to open the King's Room one morning and then something pulled the door from the other side.' No one was in the room and it was clear that no creature of flesh and blood could have held the door then vanished so quickly.

He also reported hearing ghostly footsteps following him up the stairs on a number of occasions.

A lot of the ghostly going on at Muncaster are attributed to Tom Fool, who was the fool or jester of Muncaster and who died about 1600. Peter Frost-Pennington, son-in-law of Patrick, told me that he doesn't believe that it's Tom Fool who is to blame. 'Tom is around the castle, keeping an eye on things so to speak, but it's not him who's haunting the place.'

Tom Fool (from whom we get our modern phrase 'tomfoolery' by the way) wasn't a nice man. He used to sit by the castle and if passers by asked the way to London, he would consider whether he liked the look of them; if he didn't he would point them to the quicksands rather than the ford. There's a portrait of Tom, full of the most curious detail. It's well worth trying to work out what the rhymes mean and see if you think he would have liked you or not.

The morning I stood by Tom's portrait with Peter Frost-Pennington, he told me some of Tom's legends. He explained that Tom was certainly known of by William Shakespeare and possibly even an acquaintance except the dates (still being researched) might not match. Peter paused in his tales, apologising that the hairs on the back of his neck were standing up. He did look a bit unsettled and he put it down to Tom's presence.

Tom is supposed to have murdered the local carpenter by chopping his head off. Though one version has it that this happened in the Tapestry Room, Peter told me that it probably happened in the series of outbuildings that have been recently refurbished as a cafe and gift shop. The poor carpenter fell in love with Helwise, the daughter of Sir Ferdinand Pennington. This was such an unsuitable match that Sir Ferdinand paid the evil Tom to do away with the poor man. This he did with glee and brought back the carpenter's head to show his master that he'd done the deed.

The spirits seem to cluster in this place: The ghost of the mother of a previous owner, Sir William Pennington has been seen walking the corridors. On one occasion a female visitor was scrutinising one of the pictures on the walls when she heard footsteps coming up behind her. Thinking it was one of her friends, she started to talk to the person she sensed there. But, when she turned round, she saw no one. Then she realised the footsteps had been the sound of someone walking on a stone floor, whereas the floor was carpeted.

Somebody else appears to haunt the Tapestry Room. This room does have a foreboding atmosphere. There are many portraits and other representations of people in the room dating from various periods, but none of them are smiling. The iron fire dog that lies on the grate is in the shape of a devil's head. Peter told me that he and the other staff have often watched visitors come to the door of the room then stop and go out again, not realising why they don't want to go in, but still feeling something unwelcoming. The room often feels unaccountably cold and sometimes visitors complain to the staff about it.

Guests who slept in that room often reported unpleasant experiences. There were very often the sounds of the rustling of old fashioned skirts, but on occasions rather upsetting things happened. The late Lord Carlisle slept in the room but was woken in the middle of the night by the sound of a baby crying close to him. Of course there was no human baby near.

Other people have heard the baby crying and one of them said that while that was bad, the voice of the woman singing lullabies to soothe it was unbearable.

In the 1980s, a man called James Cartland was researching into documents pertaining to Muncaster, and stayed in the Tapestry Room. He went to bed late one cold winter night with a bunch of old letters to read. He said he'd been in bed a little while when an extraordinary feeling came over him. A muffled muttering began and a noise like a child weeping was heard in the dark corner of the room. After a time, he heard the sound of someone else entering the room and a voice like a woman trying to calm the child.

Apparently Mr Cartland's story prompted a guest from the year before to come forward. This young woman had been terrified to hear footsteps outside then the door opened. She sat bolt upright and put the light on but there was no one. She was the only person staying in that part of the castle, so the next night she was extremely frightened to hear the footsteps again. This time she heard children's voices singing softly.

After these incidents Mr Cartland found an old plan which showed that, in the middle of the last century, the Tapestry Room had been the children's nursery.

In April 1994, the Association for the Scientific Study of Anomalous Phenomena sent an investigator called Jason Braithwaite with a team to spend a night in the most haunted rooms at Muncaster. One of the team, Ian Topham, reported something strange in the Tapestry Room at 02:45. 'Slowly, a figure walked through the open wooden door and paused. It was three-dimensional but very dark. You couldn't see any features on it. When it got within a couple of feet of me it sort of vanished.'

His team mate, Melanie Warren, was coming from the King's Room. She reported, 'I saw a shadow going into the Tapestry Room. I assumed it was an investigator and I was just seeing their shadow follow them into the room. I thought I knew where everyone was so that, if an investigator was going in there, perhaps something interesting had happened.' When she entered the Tapestry Room the only person in there was a white faced Ian Topham.

Peter Frost-Pennington told me that once the haunting of the Tapestry Room became quite well known there was a flood of requests to stay in there. At first people were allowed to do so for free, but now a small charge is made.

Early in the wet summer of 1998, a group of students had come to the end of their stay and, as a good bye to Muncaster, asked to stay in the Tapestry Room. A number of them crowded in there and most of them slept on the floor. However, one lucky girl got to sleep in the antique four poster bed. After a lot of talking and joking, the group gradually became quiet and dropped off to sleep.

Although everyone else was asleep, the girl in the bed couldn't doze off. Suddenly, she felt the air above her turn cold and a great pressure on her chest. She lay there terrified and tried to wake the others but couldn't speak. After a little while the 'presence' left the room.

Previously, another group of students had spent their last night at Muncaster in the study block. This has been recently converted from some of the old out buildings. One young man woke up to find a hooded figure leaning over him. He thought it was his friend playing a joke, but when he looked to his left, there was the friend asleep in the next bed. He gathered up enough courage to look back where the hooded figure had been, only to find that it had vanished.

You may be able to negotiate permission to stay overnight in the Tapestry Room, but be warned, because of the Castle's anti intruder system, once you're in, you can't get out till morning.

The Penningtons of Muncaster, like the Curwens of Workington and the Musgraves of Edenhall, have their Luck. The Luck of Muncaster is a Fifteenth Century glass basin which was given to Sir John Pennington by Henry VI for sheltering him from his enemies after his defeat in the Wars of the Roses at the Battle of Hexham in 1464. As is usual with these lucks an inscription records

> '...*whylles the family shold keep hit unbrekcken they shold gretely thryve.*'

One of the least well known of Muncaster's ghosts, but

probably the most often seen is Mary Bragg. When I first met Peter Frost-Pennington we spent so much time talking about the other ghosts that he didn't mention her. Then a month of so later, I was speaking to one of the staff of a hotel some miles away when she told me of an experience her godfather had in the gardens of Muncaster Castle.

He was training to be a landscape gardener and one day he was working with a partner near the castle when he saw a woman approaching him across the field. As she got closer, staring intently at him, he became a little unnerved and prodded his mate. 'What's this woman doing here?' he asked. The other man looked up, 'What woman?' he replied. The woman had vanished.

The next time I saw Peter Frost-Pennington, I told him about this and he said, 'That would be Mary Bragg.' Now the interesting point is that the man who saw her has no idea who or what she was to this day, but from Peter's story, the apparition fits in very well to what is known of the ghost of Mary Bragg.

A coroner's report from 1805 refers to an inquest held into the death of Mary Bragg. Her corpse was found in the River Esk with its head so badly damaged after being partially eaten by eels that he couldn't say with any certainty what had killed her. However, Peter's research has established the following story:

Mary Bragg was the housekeeper for the parson who lived in Ravenglass. She was in love with the footman at Muncaster Castle. However, one of the housemaids at Muncaster was her bitter rival for the man's affections. One night, when the parson was away, two men called on her in Ravenglass. These men appear to have been the then coachman and the groom. They told her that her lover was dangerously ill and she should come straight away. Apparently she resisted at first, saying she would go in the morning but they told her that if she waited until the morning, he would almost certainly be dead. That persuaded her, and she went with them.

She began to get suspicious when she realised that the horse's hooves had been muffled. The coach climbed the lonely road to Muncaster and, near where the car park is today, it stopped. The two men suddenly grabbed her, bundled her into the nearby trees and killed her. There was a tall tree there then which was afterwards called Mary Bragg's tree.

The murderers took her body and buried it under some undergrowth below the terraces at the castle. They thought it would be eaten by animals and birds. However, by chance, the next day one of the farm boys was taking his cattle down that way and he found the body and reported it to the head gamekeeper.

The body was taken up into one of the summerhouses on the terrace. There was a conspiracy at the castle to keep things quiet and by the next day the body had disappeared.

It was found some weeks later in the river. Nobody was prosecuted after the inquest, but a story about the curse of Mary Bragg started to spread. It seems that everyone associated with the murder and its investigation, including the coachman, the groom and the gamekeeper, died very shortly afterwards.

People soon began to see Mary and sightings have persisted until today. There are three or four members of the staff at Muncaster who will swear to having seen her and there are reports of motorists noticing a distressed looking woman near the entrance to the castle. There are even stories of motorists thinking they've hit someone but finding no one there. Peter Frost-Pennington himself believes that he may have seen her once, flitting from near the car park to the castle entrance.

Mary Bragg's tree got the reputation of being cursed. Over the years it became old and dangerous until in the mid 1990s it had to be cut down. The problem was that no one would do the job. This is actually surprisingly common still in Britain and Ireland and there are documented reports of roads going round sacred or haunted trees in rural areas because no one will cut them down.

In the end a man was found who would do the job. Special permission had to be obtained to close the road and the operation was planned to take the least possible time. Traffic was stopped and the tree was felled. Then the contractor went on to lop off the branches with a chain saw. As he cut into a thick bough near the top, warm blood spurted all over him.

It was a hibernating bat asleep in the tree, but the blood did much to confirm the tree's reputation. In the end, nobody would buy the wood and it had be taken out of Cumbria to be sold.

Leaving Muncaster behind continue south along the A595 in the direction of Millom, however, as soon as you cross the narrow bridge over the River Esk, take the narrow road on your left.

Eskdale

This is a beautiful but twisting road where you should be careful of oncoming traffic round blind bends. Keep going, following the road along the river Esk. When you come to a T junction, turn left. Cross the river again and turn left towards Eskdale Green. You'll pass a formal stone wall then a lodge building to your right A sign tells you that this is Eskdale Outward Bound College.

From the village of Eskdale Green a very minor road leads up into Mitredale, where the river Mite has its source. At the top of this track, where you can go no further in a vehicle, is the ruin of a farm called Bakerstead.

A monstrous ghost has been heard at this place that roars and screams in agony. When it's seen, its head is reported as a white, shapeless blob. The explanation is that this is a would be robber who was killed by the farmer in the early 1800s by tipping boiling candle wax over his face.

Return to Eskdale Green and turn right onto the larger road that leads back to Gosforth, you'll come to the hamlet of Santon Bridge.

In the mid 1960s some young men from the Outward Bound College at Eskdale Green decided to camp near here one night. After they'd been asleep a little while they were awakened by all sorts of noises - geese honking, dogs barking and hysterical laughter. It was a bright moonlit night and they got up to search round the campsite. There was neither man nor beast to be seen near the place.

Irton

At Santon bridge turn left to Irton rather than going right in the direction of Gosforth. You pass by a gift shop in the middle of nowhere. The first sign you're approaching Irton Hall is a well built stone estate wall on the right side of the road. You'll suddenly come upon a right turn and see the sign for Irton Hall, and The Grey Lady restaurant.

Who the Grey Lady is, is open to question. However, there's also a lady in black said to be Ann Lamplugh, wife of John Irton. The story is that after the Battle of Hexham during the Wars of the Roses, the Lancastrian King Henry VI fled and wandered in the wilds of Northumberland and Cumberland. He came at last to Irton Hall and asked John Irton for sanctuary. Irton refused him and so King Henry was obliged to hide from his enemies in an oak tree, which is still there - now 900 years old. During the night Ann Lamplugh took pity on Henry and took food to him. When her husband found out he was furious and he locked her in the upper rooms of the pele tower. Whether he let her starve to death, or let her live her natural days out there, she now haunts the pele tower and is seen on the stairs and upon the battlements.

I spoke to the current caretaker, Stan Braithwaite, who told me a little of the history of Irton Hall. In the 1920s it was owned by the Brocklebanks who founded the Cunard Line. During the Second World War it was commandeered by the government. After the War it was opened as a hotel by two ladies. It didn't pay its way in and in the early 1950s it was bought by the Cumberland & Westmorland Spastic Society who ran it as a children's home. It operated like this until the 1980s until it was sold off and became partly derelict.

At this time a group of student nurses from Huddersfield wanted to do a ghost watch to raise money for charity. They duly arrived and Stan went to see them the next morning but there was no one to be found. When Stan contacted them in Huddersfield they told him that they'd seen a dark figure near the door to the room where they were staying and the atmosphere had become very strange. One and all they'd taken flight and left before first light. What's more they wouldn't come back for an interview they'd arranged with the local paper, so Stan and his wife had to stand in for them.

Stan has never seen Ann Lamplugh himself but he did have two odd things to report. At the time after the children's home had closed, but before it was turned into self catering units, he was doing the security rounds one evening with his wife. They were startled to hear the sound of a toy machine gun coming repeatedly from what had been the children's play area. There was no one about. Finally working up the courage to go into the room, he found the toy gun lying in the middle of the floor, but no sign that anyone had been in there.

The other inexplicable thing also came from the time the Hall was deserted. Whenever he or anyone else put the key in the ancient door, before the key was turned, there would come a loud crash from way back in the Hall. What the crash was, or why it should happen, no one knows.

About a week after my interview with Stan Braithwaite, I happened to be talking to someone about Irton Hall and they mentioned a lady, now living in Gosforth, who used to clean Irton when it was a children's home. She claimed to have seen a female ghost in the pele tower. Apparently its legs were cut off, as if it were walking along a passageway lower than the modern one. The interesting thing about this ghost is that it's only seen at a certain time of year.

The same lady also said many of the children used to see the lady during the time Irton was used as a home.

Come out of Irton Hall and turn right. Don't go back to Santon Bridge but continue on this road which eventually comes to the A595 just south of Holmrook. After about two kilometres, there's a sign pointing down a lane to your right for the historic church and cross at Irton. Turn down here and where the road gets narrow, I would advise you to park and walk. Go down a delightful lane and have the most magnificent views of the mountains crowding around Eskdale.

The church at Irton stands almost alone. Nearby is the gloomy bulk of the Victorian rectory; a large town house in the middle of nowhere. It has a certain decaying charm and you can imagine ghosts at play in the empty rooms, and white faces peering at you out of upper windows.

The chief interest in the church is the cross which stands in the churchyard as it's done for at least a thousand years. It's different to the Viking Age crosses we have seen in that it's wholly Celtic in design. It's completely in the style of the high Celtic crosses that you find in Ireland, which, of course, is just over the sea behind you.

From here, get back onto the lane, turn right at the bottom and head back to the A595. Turn right at the junction with the main road and head for Gosforth.

The South Lakes

Hotel: The Royal

A Selection of Ghosts

Tel. 01524 271217

Tariff (1999): £35

Getting there:

Go to Junction 36 of the M6 and head east. Kirkby Lonsdale is well signposted; only 8 kilometres from the Motorway. For connections to the train or by bus, you should contact the Tourist Information Centre on 01524 271437

Public Transport. Ring 01228 606000 for advice.

The Royal Hotel is a handsome rectangular building of grey ashlar blocks. Covered in creepers with a neo classical porch, it fronts onto Kirkby Lonsdale's Market Place. To the right of the regular frontage is a part that bends round the corner and looks as if it belongs to another building altogether. Inside are roaring fires and comfortable chairs in high ceilinged rooms. The bar's divided up into cosy sub bars and it's a good place to spend a few hours when the rain's pouring down outside.

The Royal was previously the Rose and Crown but after Queen Adelaide stayed there in 1840, she was so pleased with the service that she gave her blessing for it to change its name to the Royal Hotel.

The Royal is famous in Kirkby Lonsdale for being haunted by at least three ghosts. One of the most persistent is a girl nicknamed Catherine by the staff. She was seen by the housekeeper, Olive Baker, in November 1997. Olive was helping a colleague with the rooms one day on the first floor, just below the stairs that lead up to the small landing by rooms 20 and 21. The maid suddenly caught Olive's

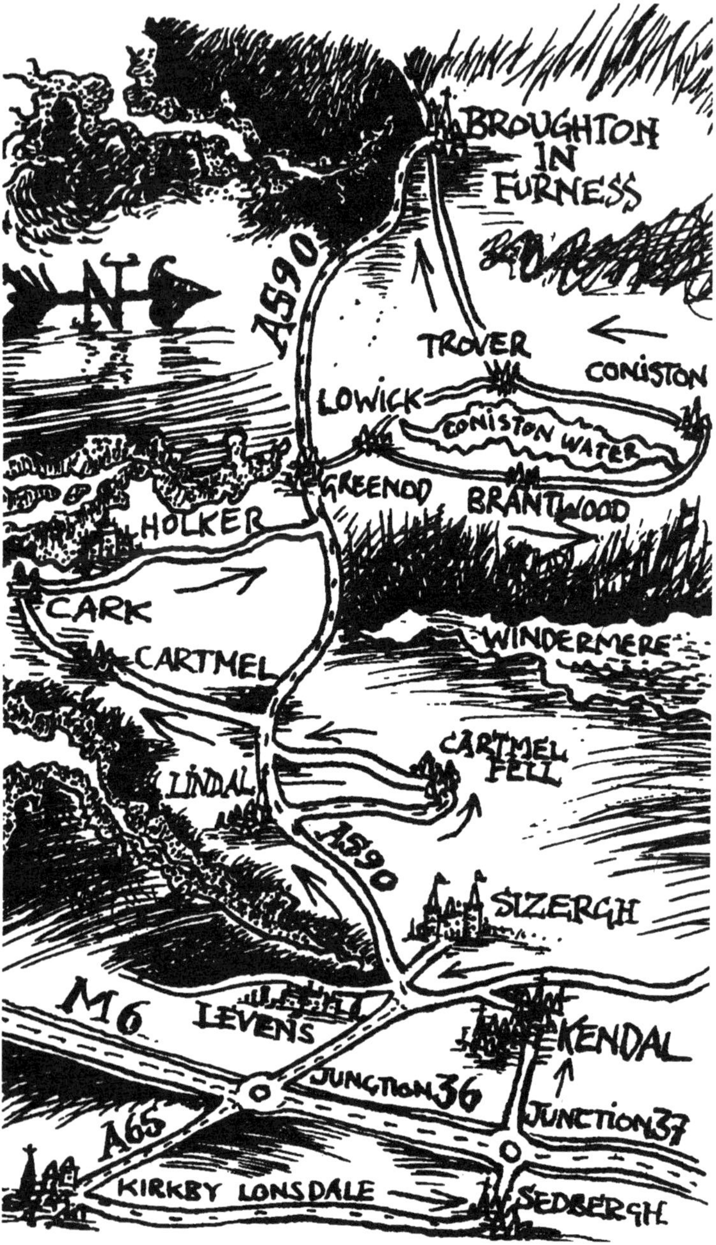
BROUGHTON IN FURNESS
A590
N
TROVER
CONISTON
LOWICK
CONISTON WATER
GREENOD
BRANTWOOD
HOLKER
CARK
CARTMEL
WINDERMERE
CARTMEL FELL
LINDAL
A590
SIZERGH
M6
LEVENS
KENDAL
JUNCTION 36
JUNCTION 37
A65
KIRKBY LONSDALE
SEDBERGH

arms and said, "Look up there!" When Olive looked she saw a misty apparition of a short woman with a long dress. She told me that she suddenly felt cold - though it was unseasonably warm outside - and her eyes began to water. "If it had been me on my own, I'd have thought I was seeing things," she said.

Though Olive had never seen Catherine before, the landing by rooms 20 and 21 is frequented by the spirit and is commonly much colder than surrounding areas. When I went up there with Olive, though I'd been warm downstairs, my back and shoulders went unaccountably cold.

Another eyewitness to an appearance of Catherine is Paul May, the landlord. One night in 1995, he was expecting for a guest. The guest had no key, so he was obliged to sit and wait by the door. It got late - about 3 a.m., and he was half dozing when he saw a woman walking through the hotel. He says she was short - about five foot two inches, with short blonde hair and wearing a traditional black and white maid's uniform. Paul told me there were only two other residents in the building that night and this woman wasn't either of them. He didn't at first think that it was a ghost, and he got up and went after her. She'd disappeared into the ladies' toilets. He went to the door, knocked, and asked what she was doing. There was no reply. He knocked again, waited and then went in. There was nobody there, and no way she could have got past him back into the hotel.

The story is that 'Catherine' is one of the five maids who were burned to death in the disastrous fire of 6th December 1820. In those days the hotel was still the Rose and Crown and the five poor girls were trapped in their rooms along the corridor on the third floor. These rooms today are numbered 7-10. The residents of Kirkby Lonsdale were so appalled at what happened that they raised a monument to them by public subscription. The monument can be seen in the churchyard; it's an obelisk which stands along the path to the left of the entrance porch to St Mary's church. However, none of the victims on the

Monument was called Catherine.

A guest who had slept in Room 6 came downstairs in the morning to complain about a persistent groaning noise that had come from Room 9. The receptionist checked and was able to assure him that there hadn't been anyone in Room 9 that night.

Early in December 1997, the chef reported a strange occurrence. He was in the hotel after finishing his shift when he smelled something burning. He thought he'd left something on the stove and went back to check, but the smell wasn't coming from there. He traced it to the corridor at the top of the building where the unfortunate maids had been 'hurried into eternity'.

Another of the ghosts is a middle aged man in evening dress with a top hat, cape and cane. He's seen on the stairs and in the area between the lounge bar and the dining room. Around this stairwell, the wood's dark and the wall paper a warm red. There's also a model of a fairground in a case by the door here with flashing lights and a revolving merry go round.

A number of residents and customers have seen the ghost that haunts this spot, but the most recent sighting comes from early October 1998. One of the barmen at the Royal Hotel is Jamie Allen. One night, about 2 a.m., Jamie had just closed the bar and was about to go up to bed. He got to the door that separates the lounge bar from the bottom of the stairs and stopped. Through the door he saw the figure of a man. At first he thought it was his own reflection, but then realised there was something odd going on. He pulled open the door; the place was gloomily lit with the main lights out but he could see a middle aged man in dark clothes coming towards him. He stood there frozen to the spot until the man disappeared into thin air. He admitted to being a little freaked out by the incident.

Jamie has also had a number of other strange experiences. Only a week before he spoke to me he'd been down in the cellar, changing barrels when, out of the corner of his eye, he saw the figure of a man. At first he thought it was Richard, his colleague, but when the figure vanished, he started to doubt himself. He got back up to the bar and asked but Richard said he'd been serving behind the bar all the time Jamie had been gone.

Paul May also told me that quite often when they're serving beer, they find that the pump has gone dead. When they go down to the cellar they find that the gas cylinders used to pump the beer up to the bar have been physically disconnected.

Jamie also told me of the ghostly snoring he'd heard twice. The first time he heard it, he was climbing the stairs with another member of staff called Joan. Joan suddenly looked at him and said, "What's that noise?" They listened and they could distinctly hear the sound of a man snoring. The trouble was there were no residents in that night. They got to the first floor landing and they found it was coming from the old residents' lounge. At that time the room wasn't in use and there shouldn't have been anyone in there. Jamie listened with his ear at the door and he could still hear it coming quite clearly from the room beyond. Looking at Joan, he opened the door. There was no one there. A little after that, the key to the room was misplaced. Once again, Jamie heard the snoring, but this time he couldn't get in to check it out.

Some years previously a member of staff and his partner had been living in one of the bedrooms upstairs. It was his habit to take off the chunky gold sovereign ring he wore and place it on the bedside table. One particular night, they were watching television when the screen flickered and then fizzled out. There was a strange atmosphere in the room and it took them some time to get to sleep.

When they awoke, they were amazed to find that the gold sovereign ring had been bent into a perfect heart shape. When they took it to a jeweller for his opinion, he said he didn't know how it could have been done without the use of sophisticated equipment not to be found locally.

Kirkby Lonsdale

Kirkby Lonsdale's wonderful place; it's a treat to wander round the cobbled streets and alleys or through the churchyard and secluded squares.

On Main Street, near Salt Pie Lane, there's an old pub called The Snooty Fox. The manager's a little sceptical of the story of the ghost, but one of the other staff told me tales of stuffed animals heads that move around. One in particular is that of a fox that launches itself off the wall. There's also a man who wanders around the back bar when the customers have gone home. It's supposed to be the spirit of a regular called Tom. Someone painted a pastel portrait of Tom which hangs by the bar where his usual seat was.

In addition to these strange occurrences in the bar, there's reputed to be a ghost upstairs who's seen in lots of the bedrooms

Kirkby Lonsdale's most famous supernatural story relates to the Devil's Bridge. The Devil's bridge is an ancient one spanning a gorge cut by the River Lune. One day, long ago, an old woman's cow strayed across the river. By the time she realised, there'd been a lot of rain and the river was running so high she couldn't cross it. The Devil appeared to her and offered to build a bridge by the next morning. His fee was the soul of the first living creature to use the bridge. She agreed to the deal and by the next morning the Devil had finished the bridge. Thinking that it was going to be her that crossed first, the Devil sat back and watched with anticipation. But the woman was smarter than he was and she threw over some bread she'd brought with her. Her little dog raced over the bridge for it and the Devil disappeared in a fit of pique, leaving the dog to his bun.

You can still see the Devil's fingermarks on the top of one of the coping stones on the east side of the bridge. Walking towards the town, it's on the top stone just past the second alcove on the left.

Follow the A684 up the Lune Valley along the track of the old Roman Road to Sedbergh. This is a Pennine town, once in Yorkshire, now in Cumbria, though I believe there's some local unrest about this annexation. Follow the A684 from Sedbergh across the M6 to Kendal (don't go onto the motorway!)

Just before you get to Kendal you'll see a farm called Capplerigg on your right. The word Capple, or Capel, is originally a Gaelic word meaning horse, but in Cumbrian folklore a cappel is a large black dog. Marjorie Rowling in her *Folklore of the Lake District* wonders if it might be related to the Cath Palug of Welsh legend. This was a huge fearsome cat that turns up in French Arthurian tales as "le chapalu". These cappels are a form of spirit or boggle that haunt the highways and byways, portending doom to travellers who see them.

Kendal

Kendal has a baffling one way system, so keep on the road until you find yourself on the long shopping street called Stricklandgate. Look out for McDonalds on your right and then on the opposite side of the road for a turning to the Marks & Spencer's supermarket. There's a public car park here.

Once you've parked, make your way back to Stricklandgate and head down the way you came. The Tourist Information Centre's on the left hand side of the road. Use this as an orientation point but then turn back on yourself and look out for an alleyway to your right. This is Angel Court and you'll see a plaque commemorating the appearance of an angel in 1745. A pub was built there called the Angel, but this was demolished in the middle of this century and the Council offices built in its place.

When Bonnie Prince Charlie's retreating troops arrived at Kendal all the citizens hid; all except one poor young child, left out alone, innocently playing. The brutal Scots were about to murder this child when an angel appeared and forbade them to do the lad any harm.

The Castle Dairy is on Wildman Street, which is slightly out of the centre of town. The best way to get to Wildman Street is to walk. Walk down Stricklandgate; head past McDonalds on your right. When you get to the first major right turn, take that. Continue along this road, over the junction to your right and onto Stramondgate. Head for the bridge over the river Kent and when you cross it you'll find yourself in Wildman Street. Wildman Street's a dark street of grubby modern buildings. It's therefore unexpected to come across such a splendid looking place as the Castle Dairy on your left. It's recessed a little from the road and made of local stone. It was a cafe but at the time of writing it's closed.

Built in 1136 on the old Roman Road, it's a Grade 1 listed building. Lancaster University says that it existed before the castle was built but when the castle was built, it was adopted as the Dower House. Over the past six years a group of Roman ghosts have been seen by customers a number of times. There's also a ghostly scullery maid and a respectable Victorian gentleman.

In *Ghosts & Legends of the Lake District*, J A Brooks reports strange goings on at The Copper Kettle, another cafe, once in Wildman Street and now closed and vanished without a trace. Apparently in 1981 there were some new owners at the Copper Kettle and they had some unpleasant experiences after locking up whereby a ghost pushed the lady downstairs. She said she could feel the imprint of the ghostly hands for hours afterwards.

A lady telephoned me and told me the story of her grandmother, Violet Vairy, who, in 1998 was 83, and who lived at a place near Kendal called Cockbeck. I have been unable to trace a place of this name close to Kendal, so it may be that the name's slightly wrong, or that the story took place further afield. In any case there was a famous ghost there known at the Green Lady and one day when Violet Vairy was five, she went to stay at the local vicarage. While she was there she developed toothache. The Green Lady came in through the window to comfort her. She saw her one other time: she was walking down a lane near the vicarage with her mother when the Lady in Green appeared. Her mother couldn't see her, but Violet could. She described her as shimmering green with long blonde hair.

There were two brothers who lived at the farmhouse near the vicarage. The two brothers both fell in love with the vicar's daughter. A feud began and, finally, when they were in her company they started to argue. This quickly became a murderous fight. The girl stepped in between them and was killed. This is supposed to be the origin of the Green Lady.

Sizergh Castle

Leave Kendal and head south on the A591. After a little while on the dual carriageway, you'll see signs for the National Trust managed Sizergh Castle. Follow the signs, past the Strickland Arms Hotel and you'll find yourself in the park of this old Lakeland house.

It's open to the public from April until the end of October each day except Fridays and Saturdays. There's an admission charge and you should telephone 01539 560070 for further details.

Pevsner calls Sizergh 'The most impressive house in Westmorland of the type consisting of a pele tower, hall range and later enlargements.' it's belonged to the Strickland family since 1239, though the house has nothing left to show from this early date.

One of the Stricklands went to war in Medieval times and left his wife behind him. He loved her but he didn't put much trust in her fidelity so while he was away fighting the Scots, he left her locked in a certain room. The servants were told not to let her go, or else he'd kill them. The trouble was that he frightened them so much that they didn't even dare unlock the door to feed her and she starved to death. Her ghost is still seen around the castle, where it wanders screaming to be released.

Another story is reported by Peter Underwood in *This Haunted Isle*. He says that in one room the floorboards are repeatedly pulled up. They have been replaced time after time but it still happens and there's no explanation of any kind for why or how.

Levens Hall

Get back onto the A591 heading south, then take the A590 in the direction of Barrow. Look out almost immediately for signs for Levens Hall. Leave the dual carriageway and get onto the A6.

Levens Hall is open to the public April until October. There's an admission charge and you should telephone 01539 560321 to check details.

As you come off the A590 onto the A6, look out for the entrance to Levens suddenly on your right. Turn in through the narrow gates and you'll see the magnificent house on your left, a wonderful Elizabethan Mansion. Levens is also famous for its gardens which were first laid out in 1694. They have been highly praised by garden experts and in 1998 won the Garden of the Year Award.

There are a variety of ghosts reported at Levens, although, when I checked with a member of staff, they said there hadn't been recent sightings of any of them.

Inside the house there's a black, shaggy dog that runs around the feet of guests, tripping them up. Guests usually think the dog belongs to other guests or the house itself, but of course it doesn't. Spirits of black dogs are particularly common in Cumbria, but they're usually of huge size and inspire dread in those that see them. This dog has been seen over the years by many well known guests who have stayed at the Hall. The dog's also supposed to be seen on the road outside the Hall and it's a dangerous distraction to drivers. Again, this is reminiscent of the various other black dogs seen at places like Shap and Caldbeck.

There's also a pink lady seen around the house wearing a dress with a pink print pattern on it.

The ghosts in the park outside the Hall are a little more sinister. One of them is known as the Grey Lady and she's supposed to be the spirit of a poor gypsy woman who came looking for charity and was left to starve at the gates. With her dying breath she cursed the owners of the hall, the Bagots (who still live there today), and said there would be no heir born to them until the river Kent stopped flowing and a white fawn was born in the park. In fact, there were no male heirs until 1895 and in that year, the Kent froze over and a white deer was born. Even though the curse is lifted, members of the family still see the Grey Lady. The last reported sighting of the poor gypsy woman was in 1954 by one of the daughters of the family.

Cartmel Fell

Rejoin the A590 in the direction of Barrow. Keep on this road until you get to a village called High Newtown. There are signposts pointing right to Cartmel Fell.

Gerald Finder records the story of charcoal burners from Cartmel Fell. One young charcoal burner was about to get married to the love of his life but as he watched the turf mound smouldering away, he was struck by a freak bolt of lightning and killed. His fiancée was called Kitty Dawson and after his death she went to the hut where he'd lived and never left it again. The neighbours were good to her and brought her blankets and food, but she was broken hearted and had no interest in eating or warming herself. In the end they found her dead. Her ghost still haunts the spot, sitting on a stone, calling his name.

The historic village of Cartmel should not be missed. It's a little way from Cartmel Fell. To get to Cartmel, go back to High Newtown, cross the A590 and go down one of the narrow roads from the other side of the road that lead you to Cartmel.

Find somewhere to stop and get out to walk around the village centre. Cartmel has a claim to be one of the most delightful villages in Cumbria with its small streets, its interesting old buildings and the lovely beck (the River Eea) that runs through it, criss crossed by ancient bridges.

Cartmel's famous for its horse races, its toffee and its ancient priory. It's recorded that the Cartmel peninsula and all its Britons were given to St Cuthbert in the eighth century so there has been a church or priory here since Anglo-Saxon times. The present church has some well preserved Norman features.

You'd expect there to be plenty of ghosts in Cartmel because of its long history and association with the priors and there have been many sightings of a ghostly figure in the lanes around the Priory and especially near the medieval gatehouse next to the building used as a tourist information centre. One of the ladies in the tourist information centre told me that footsteps had been heard on the stairs when there was no one there and dogs have been known to begin to growl or simply refuse to climb the stairs. The figure, when he's seen, is described as being middle aged with a tall hat and a double breasted waistcoat. He has the disconcerting habit of vanishing in front of those who see him.

To the east of Cartmel village is Hampsfield Hill which has a mysterious modern ghost story.

I was contacted by a man called Williams from Scotforth near Lancaster who used to walk frequently in the South Lakes area. One summer day in 1990 Mr Williams was walking with his wife and another couple. They had the Ordnance Survey map and were looking for the ruins of the medieval hospital that are marked on it. But the day wasn't so good and there was a bit of mist around. From the map, they knew that there was a right of way leading left from the path they were on but they couldn't see it.

Mr Williams became aware of a figure behind them. He glanced back. There was a tall woman dressed rather inappropriately for the fells in a long black robe. As he looked, she stopped and slowly lifted her arm to point left. All four of them saw her, but they didn't want to stare so they turned round. Mr Williams felt that she'd been pointing the way to the ruins of the Hospital. He checked the map and was certain that she was right; they'd gone past the turning. He looked round again but the woman had vanished. He told me that he suddenly suspected that something odd was going on so he ran back to where the woman had been standing. He said there were no footmarks. However, just at the point where she'd stood was the turning for the Hospital.

Pointing the way to a group of walkers seems a fairly unimportant task to bring a spirit back from the Middle Ages, and Cartmel was a Cistercian House; the Cistercians didn't wear black; the Black Friars were the Augustinians. Despite that Mr Williams had no reason to make such a story up - so who the woman was, we don't know.

Holker Hall

Go through Cartmel heading for the village of Cark. At Cark, turn right and you'll soon see signs for Holker Hall on your left.

Holker Hall's famous for its gardens and is the home of Lord and Lady Cavendish. It's open to the public from April until October and in 1998 an adult ticket cost from £3.35. If you intend to visit the award winning gardens, the deer park or the lovely house, you should contact the Hall itself to check opening times and admission charges. The telephone number is 01539 558328.

The Hall's four hundred years old and though it's

belonged to three families, culminating in the Cavendishes today, it's never actually been bought or sold.

You've come through the village of Cark, and in 1809 the owner of Cark Hall, was a well known local historian called Stockdale. One night he sent a servant boy up the road to Holker Hall with some newspapers for the Cavendishes. When the boy eventually returned he collapsed on the kitchen floor. He looked in a bad way and, as the servants gathered round him, he explained he'd run all the way back from Holker because a dobbie was after him. This dobbie, had taken the form of a ball of fire. The boy's story wasn't believed and he became something of a laughing stock.

However, about eight years later Mr Stockdale's brother had a similar experience. On the same road to Holker, he became aware of a glowing ball of fire following him. As it gained on him he realised it was the dobbie and broke into a run to escape.

From Holker, go up the BB5278 to rejoin the A590. Continue west on this road in the direction of Barrow. At the village of Greenodd, turn right and go onto the A5092. After a few kilometres, you come to the hamlet of Lowick Green. Turn right here onto the A5084 then leave the main road and head on the minor road which goes on the east side of Coniston Water.

Brantwood

Brantwood was the residence of John Ruskin the famous aesthete and art critic. Ruskin's actually buried at Coniston and there are no ghosts that I know of on this eastern bank of Coniston Water, but the beauty of the place makes up for the lack of spirits.

Brantwood's open to the public all year and has lots of memorabilia to do with Ruskin. It's also the venue for art exhibitions and for theatrical events. In 1998 an adult admission was £3.90. You should telephone 01539 441396 to check details. There's a tea shop here called Jumping Jenny's which bakes its own cakes and offers log fires or a sunny terrace depending on the season.

Continue north until you reach the top end of the lake. Turn left here onto the B5285 for Coniston

Coniston

Coniston may look like tranquil rural backwater but its important copper mines once made it a major industrial centre. The craggy mountain that looms over the village is Coniston Old Man; it's riddled with old mine workings and some of them have a sinister reputation.

In Germany, the miners used to believe that mines were the abode of kobolds. Similar tales are told of these Cumbrian mineworkings in the heart of the Old Man. The mountains west of Coniston can be very wild. There's a small tarn up in the mountains called Goat's Water, reputed to be the haunt of elves and giants that are seen around the ruinous heaps of rock in poor weather or at dawn or dusk.

If you want to cross from this part of the world to the coast, one way you can do it is to travel north to the Langdale Valleys and then over the Wrynose and Hardknott Passes. This road's rightly closed in conditions of wind, ice, fog, snow or heavy rain - it's so narrow and twisting, with precipices all around, that it can be lethal for the unprepared driver.

One mountain between the Wrynose and Hardknott passes is called Swirl How. On the Coniston side of this mountain is the feature known as Simon's Nick which looks like someone has sliced off the rock face with a knife. This whole area's full of potholes and abandoned mineshafts. It was here that a copper miner called Simon struck a deal with the Devil. According to one version of the story, Old Nick led him to a rich vein of copper but, because the Devil's a tricky person to deal with, Simon never had any benefit from it and mishap followed mishap until he was finally blown up in an explosives accident. Climbers in the area have subsequently seen Simon's ghost about the place.

In the crags above Coniston village there's a tarn called Levens Water which is supposed to have an ancient hairy trout in it. This trout's bigger than any other ever seen. Actually, the story of an ancient and wise fish crops up a number of times in Celtic and other mythologies. In Ireland the ancient salmon, Fintan, ate the nuts from the tree of knowledge and became very wise. He was later caught and cooked by Fionn Mac Cumhail who inherited his wisdom. According to the Welsh medieval tales called the Mabinogi, one of the oldest animals is the salmon of the lake known as Llyn Llyw. Only this animal knew where the god Mabon was held prisoner. What the hairy trout of Levens Water knows is still his secret.

From Coniston, head south-west on the A593 in the direction of Torver. This beautiful road brings us to the village of Broughton in Furness

Broughton in Furness

Hotel: The Old King's Head

Ghostly Caresses

Tel. 01229 716293

Tariff (1999): £18-30 B&B

Broughton in Furness is one of the most pleasant and also one of the least known small country towns in the Lake District. There are lots of slate built houses of considerable age and a delightful square with trees at its middle and interesting pubs and cafes all around. All of the streets round about the Square are worth exploring.

The Old King's Head is a long building on Church Street. The earliest record of it's in 1610 when it was known as the Kirkhouse. As soon as you step inside, if you ignore the paraphernalia of a modern pub, the dark wood, beams and low doorways show instantly how old the place is.

At the time of the first records the building belonged to the Church. Though it may seem strange for an inn to be associated with a church, it was actually quite common in remote country districts for the benefit of worshippers coming from afar. It was also useful to have an inn near to the church for use at times of weddings and funerals.

The ancient agricultural hiring fairs were held outside the King's Head each quarter day: Lady Day (25 March); Midsummer Day (24 June); Michaelmas (29 September) and Christmas Day (23 December).

About 1760, the Kirkhouse was renamed The King's Head. Though there's a tradition that Charles I once slept in the Inn, 1760 was the date of the accession of 'Mad' King George III to the throne and the name change might have been to celebrate that. By as early as 1783 it had become the 'Old' King's Head (or as it's actually recorded ' *t'ald King's Heead*'). The new King's Head was on Market Square, now the Manor Arms.

The Old King's Head was Broughton's posting house and a post chaise, car and horses were kept there. The Mail coach from Ulverston to Whitehaven called there. There was also a coach which ran to Kendal.

On the first floor, until very recently, there was a large room which has now been converted into bedrooms. The ceilings of the divided room still show the plaster mouldings of this large room which dates from the late 1700s.

It's known that the room was used for gatherings, dances, meetings and suchlike. At one time it was Broughton's theatre and companies of strolling players called there and put on plays for the townsfolk.

Ghostly happenings have been reported from Room 5. This is a strange room and you have to go through an outer door with a little step before you get to the room door itself. There's a small lobby area outside and from this an old staircase winds up. The doors are small and the wood's old and dark. Oddly, in the lobby area there are what look to be coat pegs, probably dating from the early to middle years of this century. The likely explanation is that this was the cloak room for the large function room.

Room 5 is a small room, not the best in the hotel, but certainly the most interesting from a ghostly point of view. There's a spirit lurking here. She's female and has the unnerving habit of stroking your brow with cold dead fingers as you sleep. There's never a suggestion that she means any harm; it's just a rather disturbing way to wake up.

There are also reports of something in bathroom down the hall from Room 5. The current manageress told me that the bathroom had an odd feel to it. She also told me that things keep disappearing; small things without any real value that go from places where no one but her and her husband can get to.

The electricity in the hotel also does odd things and one night the television set in their private rooms came on by itself in the small hours.

In an old place such as this you would expect creaks and groans, but they seem to be louder and less natural than normal. As well as this, I am told that doors have a habit of coming open on their own.

To finish this itinerary, you can either stay in Broughton and then do the Western Lakes itinerary by taking the minor road north west up the valley of the River Duddon to Ulpha and across the fells to Eskdale. This is well worth doing for the scenery alone, but should not be attempted in adverse weather conditions. Otherwise you can return east to Kendal and the motorway.

Though there are lots more ghosts in Cumbria than I have mentioned in this book, it contains details of all of those that I've been able to find out about that were in public places. Those ghosts which are in private houses are best left to their owners, and their owners guests. If you've not yet been to Cumbria, I hope you're duly inspired by these tales, and if you have, I hope you enjoyed this most beautiful corner of England and are planning to come back some day!

Further Reading

A History of Overwater Hall: Stephen Bore
A Literary Guide to the Lake District: Grevel Lindop
Buildings of England - Cumberland & Westmorland: Nikolaus Pevsner
Castles of Cumbria: M J Jackson
Dalston Hall Hotel History: Dalston Hall Hotel
Dictionary of Celtic Mythology: Peter Berresford Ellis
Eden Tapestry: Charlie Emett
Ghosts & Legends of the Lake District: J A Brooks
Ghosts of the Lake Counties: Gerald Findler
Ghosts of the North Country: H Tegner
Gods & Myths of Northern Europe: H R Ellis Davidson
Lacy's Caves & Long Meg: East Cumbria Countryside Project
Memories of the Cumbrian Fells: J W Roddam
Monks & Mysteries: East Cumbria Countryside Project
Pagan Celtic Britain: Anne Ross
Round Carlisle Cross: James Walter Brown
Secrets & Legends of Westmorland: Dawn Robertson
St Cuthbert's Church, Edenhall: W T McIntire
Strange But True? Casebook
The Folklore of the Lake District: Marjorie Rowling
The Good Ghost Guide: John Brooks
The Gosforth District: C A Parker
The Green Man of Carlisle Cathedral: Thirlie Grundy
The Northern Counties to AD1000: Nick Higham
The North of England Ghost Trail: Liz Linahan
The Stone Circles of Cumbria: John Waterhouse
This Haunted Isle: Peter Underwood
Trioedd Ynys Prydain - The Welsh Triads: Rachel Bromwich
Twilight of the Celtic Gods: David Clarke & Andy Roberts

Index

TOURS

The author leads tours of some of the sites mentioned in this book. These are for medium sized groups following a standard itinerary based on the itineraries in this book and taking a week to go around all the sites, or they can be put together for individuals or small groups of friends taking in those sites and themes which particularly interest them.

For further details, please contact:

The White Rabbit Press
23 Castle Terrace
Penrith
Cumbria
CA11 7DY

Notes

Notes

Notes

Notes

Notes